Betty's wisdom, down to earth attitude and sense of humour come across clearly through the pages of her book.
PSYCHIC NEWS

My Life as a Medium is crammed full of amazing case histories and experiences.
MANCHESTER EVENING NEWS

MY LIFE AS A MEDIUM

Betty Shine

Thorsons
An Imprint of HarperCollins*Publishers*

Thorsons
An Imprint of HarperCollins*Publishers*
77–85 Fulham Palace Road
Hammersmith, London W6 8JB

1160 Battery Street
San Francisco, California 94111–1213

Published in hardback by Thorsons 1996
Paperback edition 1997

1 3 5 7 9 10 8 6 4 2

A catalogue record for this book
is available from the British Library

ISBN 0 7225 3316 0

Printed and bound in Great Britain by
Caledonian International Book Manufacturing Ltd, Glasgow

Names have been changed to protect the privacy of the people who have allowed me to tell their stories.

I dedicate this book to spiritual mediums around the world. Long may they continue to spread the word and demonstrate their very special talent.

I am the daughter of Earth and Water,
And the nursling of the Sky;
I pass through the pores of the ocean and shores;
I change, but I cannot die,
For after the rain when with never a stain
The pavilion of Heaven is bare,
And the winds and sunbeams with their convex gleams
Build up the blue dome of air,
I silently laugh at my own cenotaph,
And out of the caverns of rain,
Like a child from the womb, like a ghost from the tomb
I arise and unbuild it again.

PERCY BYSSHE SHELLEY 1792-1822

CHAPTER ONE

VALERIE SAT IN THE CHAIR OPPOSITE ME in my healing room, and sobbed. I had known this would happen when the communication with her father came to an end.

She had been receiving healing from me, and as she was preparing to leave I had seen a man standing in a corner of the room. He told me that he was Valerie's father. When I asked her to sit down and explained to her what was happening, she was shocked, as she had no idea at the time that I was also a medium. Apparently, the idea of survival after death had never interested her; she had been too brutalized by this life to care about the next.

'Would you like to hear what your father has to say?' I asked gently.

'Yes,' she whispered.

'First I will describe him to you,' I said. 'He is about five foot six inches tall, of stocky build, has black hair, bushy eyebrows, a fine nose and full lips. But his eyes are his main attraction – they are twinkling and full of humour.'

Valerie nodded. Unable to speak, she had followed the direction of my gaze and was staring into the corner of the room.

'He tells me that his name is Nathan. Is that correct?' I enquired.

'Yes,' she replied. 'That was his name.'

'He is showing me a gold watch on a chain. It has a cover on the face with an intricate design and the initial "N", and was passed on to him by his father. They both shared the same name. Is that correct?'

'Yes'. I could hardly hear her reply, and asked her to speak up. She shook herself as though relieving her body of a heavy burden.

Nathan was speaking again. 'Will you tell my daughter that I love her, and that I am pleased the rest of the family were able to escape.

Death, when it came, was a merciful release, not just for me but for all of my friends who were incarcerated in that dreadful building. The shedding of the physical body was a revelation. Looking down, it seemed that a bundle of old rags was lying there, no use to anyone, whilst my real self soared into the sky. At first there was a brilliant light, then total darkness and finally a dark tunnel. Spinning through this tunnel I saw a pin-point of light, and then I suddenly shot out into Paradise. At least that was what I thought it was. My darling, you have so much to learn, and I have appeared today to tell you that you must believe in survival. Haven't I proved it to you? When you truly believe, your life will begin. Love will enter your life and you will be shown what a privilege it is to be able to give of yourself without expectancy of reward.'

There was a pause, and Nathan murmured, as though he were speaking to another presence. Still staring at the corner of the room, Valerie asked, 'What is happening?' I had to tell her that I didn't know. It must have been two minutes before Nathan spoke again.

'I have your mother here but she can't show herself yet, she doesn't know how. She hasn't been here very long.' Nathan continued, 'She wants me to tell you that we both love you very much and you are to stop crying every night because you live alone. You must believe that you are not alone – there are so many people here who give you love and comfort. You only have to believe that and the loneliness will disappear. Your aunt, Greta, wants to send her love also. I have to go now, my darling. You must believe that life is everlasting. If you do not believe that, then life will not be worth living.'

Valerie looked at me, still crying. 'Everything you have told me is true. I'm terribly lonely, I have no friends.'

'Have you ever thought about having a pet for company?' I suggested. 'There are so many unwanted animals around. And it would be a way of giving. When you are a giver rather than a taker you will find that your generosity will return to you tenfold.' Then, changing the subject, I asked her if she had recognized my description of the watch. 'Yes,' she said bitterly. 'I suppose some Nazi has passed it on to his son.'

'Valerie,' I said, 'it is only a watch. What you have received today is worth a thousand watches. I'm sorry I have to ask, but did your father die in a concentration camp?' It was quite apparent, having seen her father, that they were Jewish.

Tears were still running down her cheeks as she answered. 'Yes. My mother and I escaped with my cousins, but my father was picked up at work before he had a chance to hide.' She gave me an odd look and said, 'If I'd known you were a medium, I wouldn't have come for healing. I've always been afraid of this sort of thing.'

'Are you still afraid?' I asked.

'No! But I am shocked. However, this experience has been so beautiful I shall never be afraid again. I could actually smell my father's tobacco when he was speaking to you. Could you smell it?' she asked.

'Yes, but then I'm used to the aromas manifested by spirit people.'

We talked for some time, and when she was ready to leave she kissed me and said, 'I'm going home to think very carefully about my father's words.'

It was at this point that Nathan materialized. The wonder and joy on Valerie's face was a sight to behold. She walked toward him, arms outstretched, but as she did so, he faded. She looked at me, 'Where has he gone?' she asked.

I assured her that he was still there even though we were unable to see him, and that he must love her very much to make such a supreme effort to show himself. Valerie hugged me. 'I will never forget this as long as I live,' she said.

When Valerie had left I walked back into the healing room. It was so charged with energy that I felt as though I was walking on air. I sat down and thought about the first message I had ever received – a simple message from a mother to her daughter. Then, as I recalled the emotionally charged sitting I had just experienced, I realized just how far I had come in being able to handle the sheer power that had exuded from Valerie's father as he gave his message to his daughter.

At this point I would like to go back to the beginning of my mediumship and share the magic of my journey with you. It was not an easy journey by any means.

I had never been particularly interested in other people's lives, so one of my first questions was, 'Why me?' It was a question I was to ask myself many times over the following years. As the messages I received always made sense to somebody, I was never afraid that I was going mad. I simply was not interested, and so tried to block out the voices. Because of my lifelong interest in health, it was the healing aspect that fascinated me most – so the spirits used every opportunity to pass on messages whilst I was healing. It was almost as though they were saying, 'If you listen to us and pass on our messages we'll help you with the healing.' Oh yes, make no mistake! They were prepared to bribe me.

If I had been in a giving frame of mind it would have been easier for both sides. But I wasn't. My children had left home and, for the first time since marrying at the age of twenty, I had time to enjoy myself. Life begins at forty-five, I thought. And it did, but not in the way I had envisaged.

My main reason for trying to block out the voices was the emotional strain it put upon me. Healing was stimulating, exciting, and I had studied alternative healing for most of my adult life. I felt that I could use that knowledge in conjunction with the energies to produce good results.

Mediumship, however, was a mystery. Although my grandmother had been a medium and we all looked upon her as someone very special, it had never dawned on me that I would inherit her gifts, so I had paid very little attention to her interests. I was only ten when I was evacuated, during the Second World War, and saw very little of her from that time. The war separated many families in this way. The simple fact was that I loved being a healer but hated being a medium. Fortunately for me and for many others this changed, and this book is about my training as a medium by spirit entities.

They spent an enormous amount of time and energy dealing with my eccentricities – and I had many. Ignoring my pleas to be left alone and my threat to give up healing they continued to try to pacify me and to encourage 'survival evidence'. For this I am now truly grateful. But it was quite a different story at the beginning.

Although, I had been guided by a spirit voice from the age of two, I was still shocked when, during my forty-fifth year, my friend's late mother spoke to me and asked me to pass on a message to her daughter, who happened to be with me at the time. When I had finished relaying the message my friend looked at me and said, 'I didn't know you were a medium.' My response was, 'Neither did I!'

In my first book *Mind to Mind*, I described my visit to a famous medium and how, during the session, he had told me that I would be a great healer and that my name would become known around the world. He also explained that I was mediumistic and that I would be using this gift for clairvoyant diagnosis, amongst other things. That was twenty-two years ago, and everything he forecast has come true.

Much has been written, by myself and others, of my healing abilities, but I have never mentioned the inner conflict that I suffered as I tried to come to terms with the fact that people who were supposed to be dead were actually trying to communicate with me. And that overnight the energy floodgates had opened.

And if that was not enough, spirit forms began to build up around me. One day, whilst my daughter Janet and I were having tea in the kitchen, I happened to glance through the open door leading into a large hall. A huge funnel of blue energy had formed in the centre of the hall, and as I stared a man appeared inside the structure. He had long white hair and wore a white robe. A quick glance at Janet told me that she was wondering why I was ignoring her and staring through the door. I explained, in a whisper, what was going on and asked her to turn around. Her reaction was to tell me to close the door as she would rather not see it. I didn't, of course, as I was completely fascinated by the phenomenon. Then the entity looked straight at me with a kindly but concerned expression. My first thought was, 'If he is worried, how does he think *I* feel!' The vision slowly disappeared and as it did so I experienced a feeling of emptiness and desperately wanted it to return. It was a sensation that was to become part of my everyday life. At the time I was upset by Janet's refusal to share my experience. I was to find out much later that she had her own unique path to follow.

While I was relaxing that same evening, the faces of different nationalities manifested on the blank walls of my living room. The images vibrated as they continually changed. I remember looking at them in fascinated disbelief wondering what on earth was going on. This continued for about one hour.

Retiring to bed did not help either. When I looked up at the ceiling I could see an eye, about the size of a dinner plate. This phenomenon was something I had experienced from the beginning. It was a kindly eye, and it gave me a tremendous feeling of peace. Unfortunately, I lost a lot of sleep looking at it. It was only months later, whilst looking in the mirror, that I realized it was identical to my own; this was my mind's eye – my third eye. From that moment I was able to ignore it and my sleeping hours were restored. Three years later the eye stopped appearing, and I missed it.

Something new seemed to be happening to me every day, and there were times when I just had to get out of the house. I would drive to the nearest park and, depending on the weather, either go for a walk or sit in the car. It was on one of these occasions that I pondered over the different spirit messages I had received for myself. How was I to know whether the voices were true or whether I was listening to my own higher mind? It worried me, and I had no idea how this was going to be resolved.

The following day, whilst carrying out that most mundane of household jobs, washing-up, I had my answer. A voice repeated over and over again the christian names and surnames of both family and friends. Many of whom had been dead for some time. The repetition was extraordinary. I wrote them down. It was very similar to the way I had been taught parrot-fashion at school when learning my times table. When the voice eventually stopped I looked down at the names on the paper. Some I remembered, others I did not. As I had a day's healing ahead of me, I had to put them out of my mind at that point.

That evening the voice returned, repeating the same names three times. Toward the end many new names were mentioned. The process continued in this vein for the next two months. During that time I checked with relatives and friends, and all of the names that were unknown to me were verified. As time passed I was also given the second christian names of many of these people. Once more I had to check, and once more they were confirmed. The voice itself had no name and I was never to find out who it had been. But one thing was sure, it was the most persistent of all the communicators. If that person had ever lived on this planet he would have surely made an excellent politician!

Although the results I was having with healing were excellent, I found the survival evidence intrusive. Somehow it did not seem to belong in the healing room, although the messages were well received. But I was unhappy about it. There were so many lessons to be learnt as far as healing techniques were concerned and I needed the time to study them.

I remember sitting alone one evening, praying for the voices to stop. I had heard a child's voice that day asking to speak to her mother, and the shock had reduced me to tears. This is how it happened.

I was healing a young woman who had been suffering with acute irritable bowel syndrome for the past two years. This was her second visit. She told me she liked being with me as I didn't ask her questions. It was so peaceful. Suddenly I heard a little girl's voice saying, 'I want to speak to my Mummy.' I looked at my patient. Her eyes were closed and she appeared to be asleep. I touched her hand and she opened her eyes. 'There is a little girl here who wants to speak to her Mummy. Have you lost a child?' I asked gently.

She whispered 'Yes,' and then incredulously, 'Can you hear her?'

The child spoke again. 'Tell Mummy that the nice lady said that I could talk to her as she is so unhappy.' I passed the message on. With myself as the mediator the conversation continued as follows:

Mother: 'I love you and never stop thinking about you.'
Child: 'I know, Mummy, because sometimes I can see you.'

7

Mother: 'Where are you, darling?'

Child: 'Well, I'm not sure, but it has lovely birds and we stroke them.'

Mother: 'Who is we, darling?'

Child: 'My friends. I have to go now, Mummy.'

A woman's voice took over.

'Hello, Jill, it's May. I thought you would like to hear from Gemma. We've been worried about you.'

Jill's eye widened. 'I can't believe it! May was my aunt. She died about ten years ago.'

May then continued, 'I look after the children, and Gemma has been with me since she arrived. She is a very happy, lively little girl and much loved. Now I must go.'

Jill was crying and questioning at the same time. I sat and held her hand.

'Why did your little girl call May "the lady" and not auntie?' I asked.

Jill wiped her eyes. 'Gemma was only two when my aunt died. She didn't know her.' She frowned then, and said, 'It is strange. Gemma died exactly two years ago today.'

I smiled. 'Obviously it was a treat they had planned for you.'

'I had no idea you were a medium,' Jill remarked suddenly. I smiled and said nothing. Jill left.

If I had been truthful I could have told her that I didn't want to be a medium. That I had found the whole session a terrible strain. I relearnt a valuable lesson that day. The truth is sometimes a cross we have to bear alone so that we can ease the suffering of others.

After Jill had left I sat alone, going over and over the conversation she had had with her daughter. The little girl's voice was in my head and I couldn't get rid of it. The sadness overwhelmed me. I prayed that the voices would stop. Two weeks later Jill asked for a healing session. Although I gave her an appointment, I dreaded seeing her again. When she arrived I could not believe she was the same young woman. The pallor had gone and her previously dull eyes, were shining.

'Betty,' she said, 'I haven't come along hoping to hear from my daughter again, I just want to thank you for the precious gift I received last time I was here.' She laughed. 'I haven't suffered with my bowel since, and I know that my daughter's visit has cured me.' As an afterthought, she went on, 'With your help of course.'

Whilst I was healing Jill, a spirit child built up in the room. It was Gemma. She was smiling, and although she didn't speak I was able to give Jill an accurate description of her. Jill never looked back. Because she now knew that Gemma still lived, albeit in another dimension, it gave her the strength to rebuild her own life.

Was I being shown the link between healing and survival evidence? Did they sometimes have to go hand in hand to get results? At the time I did not know what to think. All I knew was that things were moving too fast for me and I just could not take it all in.

One night I awoke with a start. I could hear a rushing sound, like a waterfall. Then as the sound receded I saw the most beautiful coloured pictures being projected onto the wall opposite my bed. The first scene depicted a small village with white houses and a dusty track. Behind the village were hills, and just above the hills was the most beautiful sunset I have ever seen. The sky was a mass of many different colours. As I stared, the scene slowly changed. This time it showed a valley filled with people crouching on the ground, obviously listening to the figure standing before them. I could not see the face of the figure as it was half hidden by a white cowl. The scene changed again, and before me was a beautiful waterfall and the same rushing sound that I had heard on awakening. And then a voice said, 'Everything is possible.'

As my bedroom returned to normal I tried to leave my bed. At this point I needed to make myself a cup of tea – perhaps with a tot of brandy! But I could not move. The whole of my body felt like lead. Eventually, I was able to sleep. The leadenness, I was to find out later, was due to the mind energy having practically left the body, as it does with shock or deep sleep, and until it slips back, the physical body is helpless. These visions have continued, and all have a spiritual significance. I love them and would hate them to disappear altogether.

It seemed that the more I tried to reject the voices so eager to pass on messages of survival, the stronger they became. Healing sessions were usually of an hour's duration. I felt that anything less than that would lead to a sense of urgency, and when people are ill they need time to talk. When survival evidence came through, the session obviously went on for much longer and this worried me a great deal, because my clients liked the confidentiality that I gave them. I did not favour the packed waiting room. It might give the appearance of being successful, but it does little for the sensitivities of the people who are forced to share their space when they are at their lowest ebb. As I could not stop the flow of spirit voices I had to arrange my diary accordingly so that my appointments did not overlap.

This worked quite well until four friends, who all had health problems, asked if I would mind if they stayed together whilst they each received healing. I reluctantly agreed, although I thought at the time that the room was far too small for all of us. It seemed, however, that the spirit world thought it could hold a few more! As I healed, survival evidence poured through. It must have looked as though I was giving a command performance! As usual there was a mixture of tears and laughter, especially when an uncle, who had been a professional comedian, came through. His niece said, 'I cannot believe he is still telling the same old jokes.' Another of the friends had lost a watch and was told to look under the wardrobe in her bedroom. She called later to tell me that it had indeed been there. All of this happened during the evening and they were my last clients – but what if it had happened during the daytime? They had overstayed their time by two hours.

When they had gone I sat quietly in the healing room, feeling thoroughly exhausted. Leaning my elbows on the healing couch I put my head in my hands and wondered what was going to happen next. I felt that I was being knocked sideways as each individual experience gave me more problems. Then I heard a voice calling my name. It was repeated three times. Silence. A few seconds passed and the voice said, 'You must have faith, trust us.' I stood up and threw my arms out and shouted, 'Trust who? Who are you?' Silence. I was so annoyed that I began to tell them just how I felt. 'How do you think I feel?' I said dramatically, still throwing my arms around. 'Every day something different happens. I'm trying to give people privacy and then voices clamour to give survival evidence and it completely messes up my schedules, and tonight I have had to work myself to death trying to please.' Still ranting like a drama queen, I went on, 'There must be someone else you can go and bother, for Heaven's sake!' At the end of this tirade I felt wonderful, having released all the frustrations of the past six months. Perhaps that had been the reason for the silence. Nothing made me more angry than a one-way conversation, spiritual or otherwise. I had found out the hard way that one-sided conversations meant trouble. As I left the room I prayed that I would be given a peaceful night's sleep. This was granted. Perhaps my ranting had done some good after all.

Another, more personal problem was worrying me. People who I had thought of as friends were avoiding me, and one day I had the opportunity of asking one of them if there was a problem. He looked shamefaced, and told me that when he had told his mates in the pub about the wonderful survival evidence he had received they had ridiculed him. The bottom line was that he could not cope with this, and so had decided to stop seeing me. I argued that I had not changed, but was exactly the same person that I had always been. A trifle more perplexed perhaps, but the same.

'Betty, the majority of people think mediums are frauds,' he said.

'And your friends think they're the experts, do they?' I was furious.

'Why did you tell them in the first place?' I asked. 'You must have realized they would laugh at you.'

'Well, I must confess I was pretty bowled over by what had happened, and wanted to share the experience.' He smiled. 'I've been an idiot, haven't I?'

'No,' I replied. 'But I think you're being a coward.' Upset, he turned around and left.

A few months later we talked on the phone. He told me that he had needed time to think about what I had said, and laughingly agreed that he was a coward at heart.

'I am so intrigued, I can't keep away,' he confided. Eventually, the survival evidence, clairvoyance and healing won him over. He was to admit later, that it had completely changed his life. During this time there was one question that he repeatedly asked. 'As a believer, will I have to change my ways and become a goody two shoes?' 'Well if you do then I'm in serious trouble,' I replied.

It was a thought that frequently passed through my mind, especially as my clients were obviously in awe of me. Like my friend, I did not want to change. I had led an extremely eventful life and I was the sum total of every experience I had ever had. And yet the thought continued to bother me.

My mother was religious and belonged to the Church of England, and so I had become part of that Church from my birth. After much coaxing from my mother, I was confirmed in Southwark Cathedral when I was nineteen. I was already beginning to feel disenchanted and hoped by making this commitment that things would change. It is only later in life that one realizes that it is not that easy. Eventually, after much soul-searching, I stopped being a member of the Church. And from that time on, I felt spiritually cleansed. In retrospect, it is obvious that it was part of the Grand Plan that had been mapped out for me. But here I was twenty-five years later, with yet another spiritual dilemma. It had to be solved if I was to have peace of mind. And yet, as with so many problems we have during our lives, this one was going to have to be put on hold.

Throughout the first year of my mediumship I tried to make all sorts of pacts with the spirit world, some worked while others did not. I could not understand why this should be so, and continued to experiment. It was through trial and error that I began to see a pattern emerging, and this was confirmed through survival evidence.

One evening I was healing a woman who was crippled with arthritis. Halfway through the session a spirit voice told me that he would like to speak to his sister. I passed the message on and the woman was delighted that her brother was communicating. With myself acting as the mediator, the communication was as follows:

'Hello, Joan, we heard you were in trouble. I was elected to speak as we were so close when we were young.'

'Bert, it's so lovely to hear from you but who are the "we" you are speaking about?'

'Oh, Mum, Dad, Ivy, Flo and many others who loved you.'

My patient began to weep. She said, 'I am in such pain I wish I could be with you.'

'Joan, you will never be well until you have released all the hate in your heart. It is crippling you.'

'I can never forgive him for what he did to me,' she replied.

'This hate is not hurting him, only yourself.' Bert paused, then continued, 'We cannot help you until you help yourself.'

For the next twenty minutes they enjoyed a private chat about their lives until Bert said goodbye. I asked my client who the 'he' was. She told me that it was her ex-husband, and that he had made her life hell.

Joan visited me again a fortnight later. She walked into my healing room, twirled around and said, 'Look what you have done for me. My arthritis has gone.'

On questioning her about the last two weeks I found that she had rid herself of the hate she had inside her by mentally sinking into a bath and watching the black hate being released. Then she ran the water until it was clear.

'So you have actually cured yourself,' I said. She looked at me in silence for some time. 'I suppose I have,' she was perplexed. 'But it was so easy.' I smiled. 'If I had all those people rooting for me in the spirit world I would find it easy. I think the evidence you received has been a valuable lesson for both of us.'

She visited me again a year later to tell me that she was getting married and was going to live in America.

It was a simple message, but a powerful one. Working in my capacity as a medium or healer I could not always be successful if the spirituality of the client had been badly affected in some way. I began to give myself mental exercises for cleansing, and felt so much better that I passed them on to my clients. It was whilst I was sitting at my healing couch writing them down that I heard a voice say, 'We are going to try something.'

My hand moved rapidly, as I drew face after face on the blank paper. There were priests, nuns, clowns and children, and they were not all English. There were many foreign people with ornamental headdress. The drawing stopped as rapidly as it had started, and I was completely dumbfounded. I had never been able to draw at all, and here were most professional sketches. I tried to carry on, but I could sense that the force had left and with it my artistry. These sessions continued for about three weeks and I thought that I had found another talent. I was thrilled. Unfortunately, it left, one day, never to return. I found out much later that a medium is tested in many ways, and a spirit artist had obviously wanted to work through me but had found that I was not the right material. I could have told them that to begin with!

I was still being urged to give straight sittings and although my clients were extremely happy with the results, I myself did not particularly enjoy the experience. It was too inactive for me. As most of the sitters needed healing, I was able to persuade them to have healing whilst giving them survival evidence at the same time. They were delighted with the results, and this method suited me.

My mediumistic abilities enabled me to work in conjunction with a team of spirit entities, including doctors who had taken it upon themselves to train me. As in any teacher–pupil relationships we had our ups and downs. I was convinced at one stage that healing was purely magnetic, and that the spirits did not have anything to do with the healing. The team were quick to react to this.

First there was the blind man who told me that when he and his wife arrived home after healing, all the lights in their house were on, including the spare room which they never used. Also, the curtains in the bedroom were closed at night and opened in the morning.

Then a woman client told me that she had felt someone manipulating her arm in the night and found when she woke in the morning that her frozen shoulder had been cured.

A friend who suffered from migraine, mentally asked for my help during an attack. After a few minutes she felt hands on her head and shoulders and fell asleep. When she awoke the pain had gone and she never suffered another migraine.

And so it went on, until they had convinced me that there *were* spirit doctors and they did work through me. But one day whilst meditating I received this message.

Having experimented with the idea of healing being purely magnetic you have been given evidence that this is not entirely correct. But you have found out for yourself that life force is magnetic. You will find that spiritual power and life force interact all the time and it is impossible to separate the two. You were partly correct. We would like you to continue with your original ideas and when we feel that you are on the wrong path we will gently guide you back onto the correct one. You are a free spirit and will always be so.

I was glad to hear that. I hated the thought of being manipulated and sometimes the idea disturbed me. It was only the successful healings that urged me on. If so many people were being given a new life by this incredible force then what I was doing must be right. But somewhere in the corners of my mind I occasionally felt uneasy. Sometimes, I was not quite sure if the ideas I had were mine or theirs, they were so mixed up.

Other aspects were also worrying. Although I have been an avid reader all my life there were certain subjects that did not interest me, and one of those was golf. Yet when a group of friends discussed golf I found myself making suggestions that would improve their game. They were astonished, and so was I. But trying these tactics later they found them to be extremely helpful.

The same pattern was repeated whenever there was a particular topic being discussed. People who did not believe in mediumship or healing gradually began to phone me for advice, and I began to give my friends psychic consultations. Between us we monitored these consultations, which were to prove extremely accurate.

Nine months into my first year of mediumship I was to discover yet another gift. In conversation, whenever a name was mentioned, I seemed to know everything about that person and was able to give a detailed account of their personality. When asked about this ability and where the information came from, I had no answer. All I could say was that it was, 'a kind of knowing'. Now, of course, I know that it is an ability to tap the Universal Mind. Twenty-two years on I am still using this talent to help friends.

One memorable consultation was with an amateur golfer. His ambition was to achieve a hole in one. The words came before the thought as I explained what he had to do.

'Take a long look at the direction in which you want the ball to go and visualize an energy beam from the middle of your forehead to the hole. Then "see" the ball going into the hole. If you have any doubts at all it will not happen. Just "know" that it is going to happen.'

My friend laughed, 'That sounds even more difficult than trying to get it in the normal way.'

'If you simply "think it there" it should work.' We were both laughing at this point. He agreed to try, though we were both doubtful.

A week later I answered the door to find him standing there with a huge bunch of flowers. He shoved them into my arms, and raising his hands above his head, shouted, 'You're a bloody marvel. It worked!'

He then explained in detail how he had carried out my instructions to the letter and got a hole in one on the first try. Grabbing my arm he propelled me inside and told me that he wanted me to be his personal consultant. I declined. But over the years he was able to achieve his ambition five times.

I enjoyed the mixed consultations with my friends. They were always happy events and there were no great expectations, it was just fun. Nevertheless, we were all pleasantly surprised at the outcome of these meetings. For me it was a time to relax, away from the pressure that was being put upon me by requests for healing and sittings.

At the end of the first year I still found sittings difficult. The communicators themselves were very coherent most of the time, and I was at ease with the two-way conversations. The difficulty arose from the emotions that were released when the contacts came through. A sitting would sometimes leave me feeling completely exhausted.

When I had been healing it was quite the reverse and I felt exhilarated. It was to be some time before I could work out why this should be so. I was also saddened by the fact that I did not seem to have a life of my own any more. I was trying to please too many people at the same time. However, I was so fascinated by the phenomena that were becoming a daily occurrence that I could not, it seemed, cut the cord.

There was one thing, though, that angered me during this period, and that was the intolerance shown to mediums and healers. The word 'medium' seemed to bring out the worst in people. I was 'told' by Christian friends that the devil was speaking through me. I replied that if that was the case then he was pretty well informed and extremely intelligent.

'Of course he is,' was their reply. 'That is why he is so good at hoodwinking people.'

'You know him personally, do you?' I asked.

'Yes! We know him as well as we know Jesus Christ,' they said.

'Describe him,' I asked. They faltered, and then said, 'He can take on any image.' Laughing, I remarked that he must be very talented. They were furious. 'We're trying to help you. This is no laughing matter.'

'If you are right, then why does he give so much pleasure to so many people?'

They were angry, and tried to interrupt but I held up my hand to silence them. 'No, hold on,' I said. 'All the messages I have passed on to people from relatives and friends have given them such happiness. In fact they have all told me that it has changed their lives for the better. In many cases it has taken away the fear of dying.'

'They are being lured away from Christ,' they replied.

I tried to bring some logic into the conversation. 'If the church preaches that there is a life after death, then surely it should not be too much of a surprise to anyone that the survivors try to contact us to confirm this.'

'We have already told you, it is the devil mimicking them.'

We had come full circle and I decided to end the conversation. It was then that they attacked the healing. 'You can only be healed by a priest,' I was told. It did not seem to matter to them that the priest giving the healing may not be a natural healer. 'Jesus Christ would be working through him,' they said.

'But surely the Church preaches that Christ is within all of us,' I remarked.

'He is,' was the reply. 'But he will only work through those who have been ordained.'

I suggested that we should stop at that point, and they left. I believe that everyone should have their own point of view as long as it makes them happy, and I do not believe that you should try to force your opinions on others. This usually brings unhappiness.

I had been thoroughly grounded in the church's teachings, and many of them did not make sense to me. The spirit teachings did. The healing continued, and so did the mediumship. I did not know then that the second year was going to be even more incredible than the first.

CHAPTER TWO

A T THE END OF 1973, my energy had increased one hundred per cent. I felt like a time bomb waiting to explode. Subtle, yet tenacious, the spirits were there watching, guiding, protecting and, at times, an absolute pain.

My personal belongings were beginning to move around the house of their own accord, and sometimes disappeared altogether. It was frustrating and time consuming trying to locate them. Like naughty children, the spirits seemed to be testing my patience, and I could see no sense at all in their behaviour. If there were mischievous entities trying to lighten the atmosphere they did not succeed, and their actions always made me angry.

I confided these peculiar happenings to a friend who was helping with some odd jobs around the house. He laughed, and told me that it was just my imagination. When he next looked for his toolkit it had gone, and he accused me of having moved it. I assured him that I had done no such thing and we spent the next hour searching for it, but to no avail. He was extremely agitated by this time and went back into the room in which he had been working to fetch his coat. There, in full view, was his toolkit. Sitting on top of the bag was a St Christopher medal he had lost earlier that year. His face was an absolute picture.

When he left, he said, 'I will never again disbelieve the stories you tell me. Today I have had proof positive that there are things that ordinary people may never see, feel or understand, but they are there. Somehow, it's a comforting thought.' He hugged me and laughed. 'I've learned a valuable lesson today. I don't know everything.' 'Nobody ever will.' I replied.

On another occasion a female friend asked me if I could locate her wedding ring, which she had lost the previous day. I closed my eyes and asked for help in tracing it and a few moments later was given the location. It was in my own bathroom! We decided to investigate and to our amazement found the ring lying on the side of the bath. My friend was shaking. 'Betty, what on earth is going on?' she asked. 'I lost this ring in *my* home and it turns up in *yours*.'

'I have no idea,' I replied, 'This is the family bathroom. It's never used by anyone else.'

In that instant a woman's voice came through to me. 'Tell Jim he must not use his car until he has checked the brakes.' Jim was my friend's husband and I gave her the message.

'Who was she? Did she give a name?' she asked.

'No, she didn't,' I replied.

'Don't you think that is a bit odd?' I laughed, and said, 'She certainly didn't hang around, but I do think you should ring Jim and warn him.'

She did so, and a look of complete bewilderment came over her face as she spoke to her husband. She replaced the phone.

'I can't believe it,' she told me. 'He said he'd had a strong feeling that something was wrong with the brakes so he took the car to the garage to have them checked. He is waiting for the result.' My friend smiled. 'He is a real sceptic, you know. Perhaps this will make him think.' The next day she called to tell me that the brakes had been stripped on one side and could have caused a serious accident.

Two weeks later, the mysterious voice contacted me again, and told me that she was Jim's late mother. This time she wanted to give him some advice about his business. Her prophecy was later to be proved correct and prevented him from losing a large amount of money.

Whenever I felt the need to be peaceful, I would go into my healing room. By the simple act of walking into that room I was transported to another world – a world of love and beauty and forgiveness. It was so easy to close my eyes, daydream and just drift off. For as long as I can remember I have used this easy way of meditating.

One day, however, an unfamiliar voice interrupted my reverie by calling my name. As he spoke I began to feel light-headed, and felt myself drifting into a deep trance state.

'There will be great changes in your life,' he told me. 'You are being taught by the finest minds. Do not argue with them.' There was a pause, then he continued, 'The path you are on was of your own choosing.' I tried to ask questions telepathically but my mind was not functioning. When I was finally able to think logically the voice had gone.

On opening my eyes I could see a white haze swirling around the room, forming intricate patterns. It disappeared finally into a whirlpool of its own making, and I wondered whether I was being shown the door from one dimension to another.

Still feeling sleepy, I thought about his remark that the path was of my own choosing. If this was true, and there was no reason for me to suspect that it was not, why had I selected it? Why had I pursued a singing career? Why had the events of the last year all come as such a shock? There were so many questions I wanted to ask, but the answers were not forthcoming at this time. Nevertheless, I did agree with the first part of his message. It was quite obvious that I was being taught by the best when I was healing.

It was during a healing session that I was shown another aspect of mediumship. I was with a woman who had recently lost her brother. She told me that there were only three members of her family left, and that this had left her in a very depressed frame of mind. As she was speaking I could feel a presence in the room, and a man's voice said, 'Tell her it's her brother Jack.' I passed on the message, and asked whether he was the brother who had just died. She told me that Jack was her eldest brother and that he had passed on three years ago. It was Barry, the youngest, who had just died.

Jack spoke again. 'I want you to concentrate, so that my sister will be convinced we have survived.' I presumed he meant himself and Barry. Then, in my mind, I was shown a photograph. There were about ten people in the picture and I could see them all clearly.

'Tell her that she has an identical photograph at home.' I duly passed this message on, and Jack then told me that he was going to give me the names of the people in the photograph, starting at the top, and going from left to right. I told my client what was happening, and indicated that she should find a pen and paper. As the names came through she wrote them down. When Jack completed the list, he told her that everyone he had mentioned sent their love, and that she was being cared for. Tears flowed when the communication came to an end, and looking at the names, she recognized the family she had lost.

'Why aren't you in the photograph?' I asked.

'Because I took it,' she told me. 'We'd got together for my mother's birthday and I wanted to use my new camera.'

I asked whether she still had the photograph.

'I believe I have. I'll look for it when I get home, and give you a ring.' She telephoned that evening to tell me that all the names were correct, and so was the order Jack had given.

She visited me once more, for healing. As she left she said, 'I haven't suffered from depression since I last saw you, because death doesn't frighten me any more.' She held my hands and smiled. 'You see,' she went on, 'I know now that I will one day be reunited with my family, and they will be cross with me if I waste my life in the meantime.' I never saw her again, but always received a 'thank you' card at Christmas.

After this episode there seemed to be a spate of 'survivors' showing me photographs and using the same process that Jack had done. It became obvious that there must be a system of telepathy and that everyone wanted to get in on the act.

The mediumship was going very well, until a female communicator began to speak in French. When I explained to my client that I hadn't the faintest idea what was being said she explained that her father was French, and that the communicator was probably her paternal aunt.

'Well I'm afraid I'm going to have to pass on this one,' I told her. Suddenly, the aunt stopped using her voice and communicated telepathically – so the messages were conveyed and everyone was happy. I have been able to link people of all nationalities by this method. Occasionally they forget halfway through the conversation and resort to their native language, but a gentle reminder soon brings everything back to normal. There are moments when things go slightly awry, of course, but the laughter that ensues is a healing in itself.

There was one conversation that particularly moved me. It was that of a young French lady who had died in a fire. She told me that she felt no pain as the flames engulfed her because her mind had precipitated her death and had left her body before it was burned. The recipient of this message was her aunt, who was sitting beside me, weeping gently. She told me later that she had suffered terrible nightmares since the accident, supposing her niece to have died in agony.

A very similar story was that of a young man who had fallen out of a ten-storey building after a night of drinking. He contacted me whilst his mother was receiving healing and told her that his mind had left his body as he had fallen. He felt nothing as he surveyed the body lying on the ground.

'I felt as though I was a mere bystander, looking at a stranger,' he told us.

These stories have brought great comfort to those whose family and friends have died in similar circumstances. The mind protects and leaves when physically all is lost.

I was beginning to enjoy the survival evidence I received whilst giving healing. It was obvious that it brought enormous relief from pain and suffering and was, in fact, an alternative method of healing.

I was also perfecting the art of meditation, and through it was given an insight into another dimension. I had already seen a little of it as a child but now, years later, it was as though I could walk on air and I seemed to float effortlessly over mountains and valleys. I was taught that the thought was the deed. Simply think yourself somewhere and you were there. The temperature around me never changed, whether I was in a green valley or the desert, and it was always comfortable. I felt as though I was being bathed and massaged by the warm air around me, and the atmosphere was always charged with a vibrancy that one never experienced on earth. The colours were as I remembered them from my childhood. There was a brilliance, even in the pastel shades, that was hypnotic, and the perfume-laden air was intoxicating. When I was not in a meditative state I questioned whether these journeys were real or imaginary. In my heart I knew they were real, but how could I be sure? I did not want to fool myself. It was to be months before I was given the answer.

One day I slipped from a meditative mood into a trance, and found myself walking through seemingly endless corridors. The walls and ceiling of the building were transparent, and emanated a silvery light. As I reached the end of the corridor I saw my mother waiting for me. Other family and friends gathered round and we hugged and kissed. I remember asking if this was real and my mother told me never to doubt it. I wanted to stay but was informed that I still had a lot to do. When I finally awoke I knew that I had indeed been with my family and friends.

On subsequent visits I was shown halls of music, where each tone was matched by colours cascading down from the ceiling like a water-fall. I was shown how one can, with the necessary talent, think a building into existence, or think a bowl of cherries onto a table. The examples were endless and I was always enthralled at the visions before me.

These were to be confirmed time and again by survival evidence. I was entertaining some friends one evening when I saw a woman standing behind one of my female guests. I described the lady and gave her name, and was told that it was an aunt who had been dead for some time. My friend asked why her aunt was here.

'I want to tell you that I shall stay with my father until it is time for him to come with me,' was the reply.

'How long will that be?' my friend asked.

'A few days,' her aunt said. 'He will feel no more pain.' Then she left.

I thought it strange that my friend seemed happy to receive this message until she explained that her grandfather had suffered so much in the past year that death would be a merciful release for him.

Her grandfather indeed suffered no more pain, and died three days later. Proof that our loved ones ease our last moments and help us on our journey was given to me in so many ways.

I was once visiting an elderly lady in hospital when I saw a female spirit sitting at the bottom of the bed. She told me that she was waiting to take her mother 'home'. I asked the patient if she had any family.

'No!' she said. 'I did have a daughter, but she died in her teens. I'm sure I shall see her again.' I described the visitor, and she confirmed that it was her daughter.

'I expect she has come to fetch me,' she said in a matter of fact way.

'Or to give you reassurance,' I suggested, trying to be positive. The old lady smiled knowingly. 'I think she knows best,' she said. She died a week later.

A small boy, who was in the last stages of cancer, came to me for healing. Ten minutes into the session a man stood in front of me, told me that he was the boy's grandfather and that he would like to speak to his grandson. I asked the parents if they would permit me to pass on the messages. They agreed, and told me that they had spoken to their son about the afterlife, and that they believed his grandfather would be waiting for him.

'I have come to tell you how beautiful it is where I am living now,' the grandfather said. 'I had never seen real colour before I came here. And the birds are magnificent, they look like a firework display as they move through the air. There are animals everywhere and they are loved by everyone.'

'Will I be with you?' the boy asked.

'Of course,' he was told. 'I can't wait to show you around. I must go now. Be seeing you.'

The parents tried to hide their tears for the sake of their son. They were still hoping for a miracle cure, but knew that they had just been given the answer. The little boy was ecstatic. He could not wait to see his beloved grandfather again, and spoke of nothing else during the remainder of the healing.

He died two months later. His mother told me that he had held conversations with his grandfather whilst in a coma. 'There is no doubt that he could see and hear him,' she said. The grandfather had arrived to ease the boy's last days on earth, and had also given the parents immense pleasure knowing that he would be waiting for their child. But most of all it had relieved them of much pain and despair. Through the power of mediumship they had received a miracle.

It was at times like these that I realized the importance of mediumship. It is a talent that goes beyond anything that can be given by other professionals, and is a vital link between two worlds. With it comes a responsibility that can make or break you. 'Is that what is happening to me?' I asked myself. 'Am I being tested to find out whether I can survive the onslaught?' In the past 18 months I had certainly experienced phenomena that were absolutely incredible.

At times I found the whole process quite unbelievable. I had never had any inclination to involve myself with the paranormal in any way; my life had been too full of other interests and I knew nothing of spiritualism. The idea of visiting a spiritualist church would have been entirely alien to me.

However, I was taken to several spiritualist churches by a friend who thought that it would ease my path and provide some of the answers to my innumerable questions. But I soon closed that particular door, realizing that I had to find out the truth about this very extraordinary profession, for myself. I decided to follow a solitary path, mainly because I did not want to be brainwashed by the thoughts of others. If this was to be my future, and it was certainly beginning to look as though it was, then I had to break down all the barriers and come face to face, not only with myself, but with the power behind the phenomena.

One particular episode taxed my imagination. A small boy, who had been receiving healing from me, told his mother that he had seen me sitting on his bed during the night. 'She was wearing a long blue gown, and smiled at me,' he said, and though his mother questioned him for some time, intimating that he could have been dreaming, he was adamant. 'I know I wasn't dreaming because she woke me up when she sat on the bed.' When his mother told me the story I was nonplussed. As far as I knew I had been safely tucked up in my own bed.

A similar story was given to me by another patient. Her husband was in a London hospital suffering from emphysema, and she had asked me to give him absent healing. When she visited him the following day he told her that a blonde woman wearing a long blue gown had visited him during the night. She asked him for a description, when he gave it, she said, 'Oh, that's Betty,' and explained that she had asked me to give absent healing. She could not contain her excitement when she recounted the story to me. 'How do you do it?' she asked. I could only tell her that I hadn't the faintest idea.

These nocturnal 'visits' were to become a regular occurrence, and were a complete mystery to me until a familiar voice – who I was by now calling my guru – told me that the mind leaves the body in sleep and can move around freely and show itself as a spirit form, exactly the same method as when someone dies and then appears as a spirit.

'But how can these people see me when they're awake?' I asked.

'Because their mind is still partly out of the body. We can only be seen with the mind,' he answered. 'Mind energy consists of the same elements as our dimension.' It was a relief to know that somewhere, somehow, I was not harbouring a strange wardrobe and wandering about at night. Obviously my mind had a mind of its own!

One evening, feeling particularly drained after a full day's healing, I sat down in my favourite armchair and drifted off into a light sleep. I awoke with a start when I felt the pressure of hands on my shoulders, but although I looked around there was no one there. I stood up and searched every room in the house, but I was definitely alone. I returned to my armchair, sat down and closed my eyes, and immediately felt the pressure on my shoulders again. I must admit it felt a bit creepy, and this time I simply could not move. I thought I recognized the feel of the hands but could not quite place it. Quite suddenly I was relieved of the pressure and found that I could stand. I walked around the room, feeling a bit odd, when something to my right caught my attention, I turned, and standing before me was my mother. I was so moved that I could not utter a sound. She smiled and disappeared. Trying to recall the vision later I could not remember whether she had been solid or transparent. I decided later that I had probably seen her as both as I had moved from one dimension to another.

There were times when I felt that the spirits had completely taken over my home. I would occasionally catch a fleeting glimpse of a spirit form if I turned suddenly, and it was this experience that taught me that the spirit world is not 'out there' somewhere. It is all around us. It is the energy counterpart of this planet and when we die our minds, free once more, spin through an energy vortex and, quite simply, go home.

In my first book, *Mind to Mind*, I told of the spirits that I could see walking through my bedroom as a child. Now I was being shown, once more, that this seemingly solid world of ours is but a shadow to the spirit world. That is why entities are able to disappear through doors and walls, and walk through wardrobes.

This conviction was confirmed one night when I saw the spirit form of a deceased friend quite literally walk through the wardrobe in my bedroom, sit on the bed and then it disappeared. A minute later he came up through the floor and stood laughing at the foot of the bed. I could sense him saying, 'Well, what do you think about that!'

I found it quite extraordinary that I was accepting these visitations so easily – a far cry from my childhood when I habitually walked backwards, bumping into everything, because the church had convinced me that the devil was following me and waiting to pounce if I misbehaved. At least that is how my young mind interpreted it. And I hated the idea of a guardian angel. It sounded so GOOD! The entities that shared my life now were normal; there was no goody-goody stuff with this lot, they were just ordinary beings going about their lives, albeit in another world. I was finally beginning to like the 'feel' of this new experience, and loved the warm embrace of the energy that surrounded me, especially when I was healing.

All my life I had felt that there was something wonderful waiting to happen. When I fell in love I used to think, 'This is it.' But after a while I would realize that it was not 'the happening' yet, that it was still to come. I used to lie awake at night sometimes, wondering what it was going to be. I would frequently stare at the night sky, seeking the answer amongst the stars and beyond, but nothing could have prepared me for what was happening to me now; this, surely, must be the supreme 'happening'.

But as in everything, there has to be another side of the coin and that for me was my continued apathy toward the idea of giving 'sittings'.

When I did give in I made sure that the room was bright and cheerful. There were no dark rooms with red lights for me – that would have totally depressed me. Although my clients were always moved and overjoyed by the outcome, I was unable to rid myself of the restlessness that I felt throughout the whole sitting. I had so much energy!

I often thought how stupid I would feel if no one wished to communicate and we had to sit in complete silence. But the challenge was to come in an entirely different way, and although I have recounted this story before I think it is still worth recalling, if only to help would-be mediums.

Within a few minutes of giving one particular sitting, I was given a picture of a pink elephant, and for a moment I wondered whether my client was an alcoholic. The picture appeared in my mind three times.

'I'm sorry I haven't said anything yet,' I told her, 'but quite honestly all I'm getting is a picture of a pink elephant.'

She was delighted. 'I cannot thank you enough,' she replied, 'that is all I wanted to hear.' She explained: 'When my husband died he told me that if there was an afterlife he would show me a pink elephant. I've already been to several mediums, and was beginning to think that there was no life after death.' She looked a little shamefaced, and went on, 'I have to tell you that I deliberately thought of something else so that you couldn't pick it up telepathically.' Then she asked me why the other mediums had not picked it up.

'There could be many reasons,' I replied. 'Perhaps your husband wasn't around to pass the message on. Or, if they *did* get the message they might have felt a bit stupid.' I smiled. 'I must admit, I thought you were going to laugh at me.'

'I'm so glad you told me,' she said. 'You've made me very happy.'

When she had gone, I wondered how many mediums had left out a vital piece of information whilst passing on survival evidence, simply to protect their own reputations. I was beginning to realize how much courage and intelligence one had to have to become a good medium. Receiving the messages was only a small part of the whole. Throughout the first two years, a pattern evolved both in healing and mediumship. A new experience would result in a spate of similar occurrences.

Whilst giving healing to a young woman, her brother came through and showed me a book with a thistle pressed in it. She understood this because he had promised that this would be his way of showing her that life did exist after death. She was understandably shaken, because she had not expected the information to be given to her during a healing session. She had visited several mediums previously, to no avail, and as her brother had been dead for four years she had completely forgotten his original promise.

On one occasion when I was giving a friend counselling, the beautiful scent of a rose filled the air. She recognized it immediately as a rose her father had loved when he was alive.

'He promised to send me a rose if he survived,' she told me, 'but the perfume is even better.' Just as she was about to leave she found a rose lying next to her handbag. It was the same variety that her father had grown and loved.

I had a similar communication whilst healing a man in his fifties. He most definitely did not believe in the afterlife, and I often pulled his leg about it. I was in a quandary. What should I do? I had to pass on the message although I knew I would be giving him ammunition for the future if it did not make any sense to him.

'There is someone here who wishes to communicate with you,' I said.

'You must be joking,' he replied. 'You're having me on.'

I smiled. 'I promise you I'm not. His name is Peter, and he's saying that he still owes you a fiver.'

'Bloody hell! That's my brother-in-law, and that was the last thing I said to him before he died. It was a joke, because he owed me the fiver since his wedding thirty years ago.'

'He's telling me that he's definitely going to return it to you, to prove once and for all that he is still alive. There you are,' I went on, laughing. 'And he doesn't like the way you speak to me about the afterlife!'

Peter then passed on several messages of a private nature, and when he had finished my patient was completely nonplussed and rather put out. 'I'm going to have to think about this before I tell the family. They'll think I've gone barmy.' 'Well, let me know if you get the five pounds,' I joked. A month later he rang and told me that when he had got into his car that morning a five pound note had been lying on the passenger seat! It could not have been placed there by anyone else as he had the only set of keys. The spirits are very fond of leaving money around for some reason and they seem to favour the five pound note. I have been the recipient of many of these notes, and have found them in the most unlikely places.

It was now 1974, well into the second year of these incredible happenings, and I was being urged by a number of people to 'take to the platform' – the platform being spiritualist churches and the like. I had already been informed by the first medium I had visited that I would not work from the platform and that my work would always be confidential. I could well understand this, as I am a very private person. I had been the grateful recipient of messages from mediums who worked in the churches, so it was not a question of disapproval. It was simply not me.

'But all good mediums take to the platform,' my friend informed me.

'Well, this one won't be doing so,' I told her. I also knew that I had a lot to learn and that I needed to do this in the privacy of my own home.

The more I thought about this issue the more important it became when I thought about the very private messages that came through, and the tears and laughter that ensued when I passed them on. There are as many people who wish to keep their lives a private matter between themselves and the communicator as there are those who do not mind sharing their messages with others. I fall into the former group, so I suppose it is inevitable that I have elected to work confidentially.

Many people believe that it is only women who seek help and guidance through mediumship, but this is not so, I had many men ask for my help. They tended to book evening appointments and I frequently worked until eleven o'clock at night. I believe that they felt at ease with me because very often the outcome of a sitting would be just as much a surprise to me as it was to them. During one of these sessions a man spoke to me.

'My name is Carl. Would you tell my son that I did not leave my wife destitute as he believes.'

The man sitting opposite me stared in disbelief as I gave him the message. Then he said, 'I'm afraid my father is wrong. We've looked everywhere for the life insurance policy that he always said existed, and there is no sign of it.'

The father spoke again. 'Do you remember, as a boy, creeping up behind me when I visited the cellar?' There was a pause as I passed the information on to my client, who answered in the affirmative. 'Do you remember what I was doing?' the father asked.

My client looked puzzled and said, 'No, I don't know what he was doing.'

It was here that the voice stopped and instead I was given the pictures of a cellar. At the side of a workbench someone was taking a brick out of the wall. A hand reached into the space and brought out a box. Then the visions ended. The son was stunned. 'I had no idea what he was up to when he went down there. The crafty old devil.'

He then told me that he had been extremely worried about his mother's future. 'Although she has her own home,' he said, 'she only has a small pension. I'm helping her, but with three children of my own it is very difficult.' He laughed for the first time. 'I hope there is something in that bloody box.'

And there was. Speaking to me a week later he told me how he had rushed to his mother's house and after a hasty greeting had gone down to the cellar. Examining the wall at the side of the bench he had found the loose brick and the box. Inside were three life insurance policies, worth in the region of eighty thousand pounds.

If he had not sought help from a medium, those policies would have remained hidden.

Every day seemed to bring such wonder to me, and I wanted to share my experiences with the whole world. But, intuitively, I knew that it was too early. Although I was a relative newcomer in this field I had already seen the destructive influences at work and I knew I had to wait until I could prove myself under the most trying circumstances. In fact, I waited twelve years. More of that later.

Occasionally, my life was disrupted by an aggressive individual. One such person was the father of a small boy who suffered agonizing pains in his legs. The mother had brought the boy to me and the pain had receded after only two visits. It was then that the father decided he did not want the boy to receive healing. He would not give a reason but threatened the mother with dire results if she brought him to me. Fortunately for her son she chose to ignore the threats and continued with the healing.

One day, whilst I was healing the boy, the front door bell rang, and continued to ring until I opened the door. A man rushed past me, opening doors until he found the healing room. At this stage I had no idea who he was. When I entered the room I realized he was the boy's father. He and his wife were having a terrible row and the child was crying, I managed to calm them down and sat talking to them for several minutes. Amidst all this confusion a spirit voice told me to get the mother and child out of the room. I turned to the woman and suggested that she take her son to my kitchen and make us all a cup of tea. She agreed. Left alone with the father, I told him that someone was trying to communicate with him.

He exploded! 'I don't want to listen to all this rubbish,' he said. 'That's why I don't want the boy coming here.' I continued. 'It is your grandmother, Mabel.' On hearing his grandmother's name he became speechless.

'She's telling me that out of all her grandchildren you were the one who used to show her kindness and respect. Is that correct?' I asked. He nodded and I continued. 'She is telling me that your aggression stems from the fact that you always longed for a child to share your interest in sport, especially football, and that you are devastated by your son's disability.' The man covered his face with his hands and quietly sobbed.

I got up and locked the door. I did not want his wife and son to see him this way. Placing my hand on his shoulder, I said, 'Mabel is telling me that she had impressed upon your wife to bring your son to me as the medical profession could not help him.' At that point the messages ended.

I waited for the man to compose himself, then said, 'Your grandmother has made such an effort to help. What is there to lose? Allow your son to have healing. You never know, Mabel may be able to conjure up a miracle or two.' He stared at me. 'But I don't believe in it.' 'Well, let my belief carry us all,' I suggested.

I left him alone for a few minutes and then returned with his wife and son. We sat in silence for a while and then, much to the mother's astonishment, the little boy's father said, 'Well, son, I think we will both be bringing you next week.' He had his reward when his son put his arms around his neck and kissed him.

Six months later they were playing football together, the child never looked back, and he and his father had a very special relationship from that day on.

On another occasion a woman arrived for healing. During the treatment I heard a man's voice saying, 'Beth, you must get out, you're in danger.' I asked my client about her home life as I felt that was where the danger lay. It became obvious during the course of the conversation that I was right, and I decided to pass the message on to her so that we could discuss it. It did not seem to come as a surprise to her at all, in fact, she was very calm. She simply said, 'I know.' I asked her why she was not prepared to leave and she told me that her husband was mentally ill and would not seek treatment. He was becoming so aggressive that she was afraid he would commit suicide.

The voice spoke again. 'Tell her this is Len, and I want her to leave now as she is making it too easy for him.' I passed the message on to her, and she told me that Len was her late father-in-law. We discussed what he had said and I urged her to leave, if only for a few days. I was extremely worried about the situation, as I could hear the urgency in Len's voice. Before she left I suggested that she should think very carefully about the information she had been given. Two days later she telephoned to say that her husband had tried to attack her so she had left and was now staying with her sister.

Three months later she came to see me and told me the whole story. Apparently, her husband had suffered a nervous breakdown the previous year but had refused to visit his doctor. He would not allow any of his family and friends to help him and had simply given up. He had lost his job, and had locked himself away in his home refusing to see anyone at all.

When Beth had returned home after visiting me he insisted on knowing where she had been and when she had refused to tell him, he became angry and attacked her. She realized, perhaps for the first time, that she was in danger, and decided to take Len's advice and get out. The outcome was that with no one to lean on, her husband eventually sought help from his doctor, who recommended counselling.

Beth told me that it was Len's messages that had been the deciding factor when she had left. She realized for the first time that her strength was encouraging her husband's weakness. Now his health was restored, they were back together, and were extremely happy.

Beth had decided against telling her husband about the spirit messages. So she was surprised one day when he said, 'You know, all the time I was ill I felt that my father was with me and was trying to tell me something. I wish I knew what it was.'

'Well, perhaps one day we'll visit a medium and you'll find out,' Beth replied.

'You must be joking,' he said. 'I don't believe in all that stuff.' Beth just smiled.

I find it quite extraordinary that thousands of people who believe their late family and friends are often around them also insist that there is no life after death. It is totally illogical. And, many of those who *do* believe will not visit a medium because they are afraid their loved ones will speak to them.

I was also astonished to find that many clients who received wonderful survival evidence were unable to believe what they had heard and half suggested that I had been checking up on their family.

I have never had the time to check my own family trees, let alone hundreds of others!

Everyone I met assumed that I had sat for years in a development group and were astonished when I told them that it had all more or less happened overnight. I am far too impatient to sit around waiting for something to happen, but when it does I take advantage of what I have been given. That is why in these first years I really had a great time. I could not wait for the next instalment, and when it came I was like a child with a new toy. I played with it, challenged it and, needless to say, marvelled at. As I did with the next experience.

I was quietly reading a book one evening and became aware of a swirl of energy around me. Placing the book on the couch, I looked around the room and found that I was in the centre of a moving landscape of colour – pink clouds, orange hills, blue waterfalls and brilliant white fountains, a kaleidoscope of different pictures, landscapes filled with the beauty of colour, moving and changing all the time. I was entranced. Then a voice said, 'Colour changes everything.' It certainly did. When the energy silently slipped away and I was left once again with my ordinary room, I felt cheated. From that day on I brought more colour into my life. I also experimented with colour healing and found that it was extremely beneficial, especially with distant healing.

Time and again I marvelled at this incredible world that was being shown to me. It made everyday surroundings appear so dull. My whole life seemed to be on a roller coaster, and there was no way that I could control the brakes. When I was tired, I often tried to shut it all out but could not. If it was not amazing phenomena it was small things, like the sound of the telephone ringing in my ears, warning me that my own phone would ring in a few seconds. Or the sound of a dog barking in my head – though we had no animals at that time. My belongings continued to disappear and reappear in the most peculiar places. This still annoyed me! There were whirlwinds of energy that felt as though someone had opened all the doors and windows on a chill winter evening. I felt a hand stroking my face whilst I was healing. I had become quite blasé about the beam of light in the hall as it appeared so often. Sometimes there was someone inside the beam but very often it was empty. I had begun to think of it as a spaceship, which was really strange as I have always been bored to tears with things like the *Star Trek* films on television. However, it was the appearance of spirit forms that held my attention. How wonderful they were! And how incredible it was to study this phenomenon that had first manifested when I was a child, when I hadn't a clue what was going on. Now, thirty-five years later, I still didn't know an awful lot but at least the added years had given me the gift of reasoning – even though that was being taxed at this time.

I remember one incident in particular. I had finished healing for the day and was just about to leave the room when I saw a spirit form taking shape from the feet upwards. This was no ordinary spirit. It was a man with long white hair, whose beard practically reached his waist. He was wearing a white gown that swirled around his feet. My first thought was that he looked like Father Time, or at least how I would have imagined him. My legs were shaking so much I had to sit down. I waited for some kind of communication, but there was nothing. Then objects began to dance around on the table and the room seemed to shake. It was scary. I was staring at the old man and our eyes appeared to be locked together in some kind of beam. Then, just like a melting snowman, he disappeared into the floor and was gone.

It was incredible to say the least, and I was longing to tell someone about it, but felt that my family and friends had already been pushed to the edge with my new found talents. I was intrigued, and for days I tried to recreate the image of this man. Who was he? What did he want to tell me? Had he been trying to communicate telepathically? I certainly did not feel any benefit from him having appeared, and had received no extra knowledge. At least not yet. It was to be a week before I found out what I had been given. Whilst speaking to a friend I realized that when she mentioned someone's name I knew everything about them. I asked her to test me by mentioning names that were unknown to me, and the results were amazing. Previously, I could give an outline of the personality, but now, I was being given minute details about their lives, and their future. Somehow, this man had given me a line straight through to the Universal Mind. It was an incredible discovery, and a talent that enabled me to help people who were unable to visit me.

One such person was a lady who was bedridden and totally dependent on her family. She wrote to request absent healing and, at the same time, asked whether I could suggest Christmas presents for two nieces and a nephew. The names and birth dates were listed at the bottom of the letter, and as I studied them I had a picture of all three children. The two girls were totally different personalities; one was rather excitable and the other quiet, and as I thought about them individually I was able to recommend suitable gifts. When I linked into her nephew I knew that he would like a dartboard.

A month later I received the following letter:

It is with great regret that I have to tell you that my aunt died four days after Christmas.

I thank you from the bottom of my heart for helping her with the children's presents. She was overcome with joy when she saw how thrilled they were with her gifts. Needless to say, the children will treasure them and they will remind them of a very loving and lovely person.

I have only one question: How did you do it? I am fascinated.

How could I tell her when I did not know the answer myself?

My life was becoming stranger than fiction, and at times I had the feeling that my home had become a time capsule. Visions of the past and future were constantly being relayed to me. The visions I did not like were those that showed disasters waiting to happen.

One night, in a dream, I saw an aircraft crash into some palm trees on the water's edge, and I watched as it crumpled onto the beach in slow motion, the blue sea lapping over the wings of the aircraft. In the distance I could hear people crying for help, and then I woke up.

I woke my daughter, Janet, and told her that there had been a terrible plane crash. I was quite distraught; the vision was still in my mind and I felt as though I had been a part of the tragedy. Although I knew the crash had happened on a tropical island I had not been given a name or a date, and it could have happened anywhere in the world. The frustration was immense. Eventually I went back to bed.

The following morning I turned on the television, expecting to hear about the disaster. There was nothing. For the next week I listened to every news broadcast, and when I still heard nothing about the crash I decided that it had only been a dream after all.

Two weeks later I was looking at the television and was shocked to see my dream being re-enacted on the screen. The plane was going across the screen from right to left, exactly as I had seen it. It crashed into the palm trees and landed on the edge of the beach, and I heard the news reader say that many lives had been lost. I was devastated. What was the point of giving me the vision if I was unable to help? Why wasn't I given the time and place so that the accident could have been averted?

Whilst meditating some time later, I was told that I was to become part of a group who help accident victims come to terms with the fact that they were dead. When someone dies in this way they cannot understand why people in this dimension cannot see or hear them because for a time they still feel normal. I asked how I could help, as it was obvious to me that the majority of relatives and friends would not be visiting a medium. I was told that I would be helping whilst in a sleep state. Although it all sounded very interesting, I still could not see how I could fulfil this role.

A few years later a woman came for a sitting and I told her that there was a young girl, Sara, who said she was her daughter. The woman held her head in her hands for a few moments. When she looked up, she said, 'I have been praying that she would contact me. What does she have to say?'

'She is telling me that she brought your attention to a newspaper article about me,' I replied, laughing. 'Why should she want to do that?'

'I don't know,' Sara's mother said, 'but she's right. Someone had left their paper on the train and I was attracted to your photograph and read the article. It was then that I decided to visit you.'

'Your daughter tells me that you have always wondered whether she suffered when she was killed in the car crash. Is that right?'

'Yes. That thought is always with me.'

'She wants you to know that she did not suffer at all.' I paused. 'That's strange, she's thanking me for easing her path and for being there when she needed me.'

The mother frowned. 'How could you have helped her?'

I explained about the activities of the rescue service. She found it hard to understand – and so did I! But this was only the beginning. There were to be many similar messages given to me in the future. That particular sitting continued for an hour, bringing mother and daughter together for the first time in two years.

At this point in time I was beginning to feel frustrated with many aspects of my life, not least the inability to find time for myself. I was now working twelve hours a day, six days a week. I tried not to work on Sunday.

Family and friends were urging me to take it easy, but what could I do when there were so many people needing help and guidance? There was already a four-week waiting list. If I cut down on my working hours that list would grow longer, and I feared for the health of some of my patients. I made the decision to reduce the hour-long appointments to half an hour.

Now, in 1975, I was in the third year of my healing and mediumship.

CHAPTER THREE

M Y MEDIUMSHIP WAS TESTED CONTINUALLY whilst I was healing. At first there was the smell of ether, so strong at times that it affected everyone visiting my home. Most of my patients claimed that it made them feel light-headed. Although I hated it, I found that in a peculiar way – it also comforted me. I felt that someone was trying to impress upon me that I was being guided. This was also confirmed by my medium friend.

'For our spirit friends,' he told me, 'it is the simplest way of letting you know that a surgeon wishes to work through you.'

'How long do you think it will last?' I asked.

'However long it takes to convince you,' he replied. On the rare occasions that we met I tried to persuade him to become my mentor, but he was adamant.

'You do not need me,' he said. 'I know that you have the finest spirit teachers available to you, because I have never seen anyone surrounded by so much power. All you have to do is listen and learn.' He leaned forward and touched my hand. 'You see, my dear, all I am is what my spirit helpers allow me to be. I am not a healer. I couldn't heal anyone. I am just a medium, and use that talent to help where I can.'

From the beginning I had felt a presence whilst healing, and occasionally caught a glimpse of spirit hands touching the patient. The first time it happened I thought my mind was playing tricks with me. The following day, when the hands appeared again I could also see the lower part of the arms. Eventually I was able to see the whole spirit entity but, unlike many mediums who have specific people working through them, I seemed to have been contacted by a variety of personalities. I wondered, if they were trying to find someone who suited my own psyche. It was very easy to distinguish between them; as their minds linked with mine their differing personalities were immediately obvious because they affected my own behaviour. One or two of the doctors had a sense of humour not unlike my own, while another would be very sombre and so the healing would be very quiet. The spirit doctor who carried out the manipulations of limbs was very excitable, and gave me the impression that he was, perhaps, slightly eccentric. I found it all absolutely fascinating.

I have mentioned in a previous book, *Mind Magic*, the time when Louis Pasteur manifested three times and informed me that he was going to help me with the healing, and of how I visited the library to find a photograph that would confirm that it was indeed that great doctor. The incredible healing that took place after this visitation was further confirmation.

I have always had a theory that if one keeps a picture in one's mind of a particular person then, eventually, that image will be played back to us. I was absolutely determined that this was not going to happen to me, mainly because I was seeking the truth.

I know the manifestation of Louis Pasteur was real, because I had not thought about him since leaving school. Although my patients often asked the name of the spirit doctor who worked through me, I was loath to mention a name as famous as that of Pasteur, so my reply was that I did not know. I was given a photograph of him by a close friend, but hid it in a drawer because I did not want his image to encroach upon my mind. I knew he would understand.

From time to time other spirit doctors have come through and given me their names, but for some reason I have never bothered to write them down. The names themselves did not mean anything to me; it was their achievements that inspired me.

I came to the conclusion, after several years, that there were many brilliant doctors helping me, but Pasteur was definitely at the helm, holding everything and everybody together.

However, in my third year I was left wondering who on earth all these people were. It was made clear to me when I began to take note of the patients and their specific ailments that the spirit doctors were specialists in their own field. Since then I always ask for 'the best you've got' at the beginning of a healing session – and I know that my wish will be granted.

I was also determined, at this stage, not to study medical textbooks. Apart from the fact that they can be extremely depressing, I do believe that 'a little knowledge can be a dangerous thing'. Imagine my surprise, then, when a medical diagnosis was given to me. Many of my patients were delighted, because they had been visiting their doctors for years without any lasting cure. Most of the diagnoses were eventually confirmed by medical specialists, but a number of my patients had vowed, before visiting me, that they would never again put their lives in the hands of doctors. Although I never agreed with this decision I could sympathize. I had been there myself, having to date been given two terminal prognoses which had eventually turned out to be common problems that could be cured by vitamin and mineral therapy. But, one must not lose sight of the fact that we could be putting our lives at risk by not taking the best of both worlds.

Jimmy's story is typical of this.

He was in his twenties, and was suffering from a dragging pain in the left side of his groin. The diagnosis I received was that it was a hernia and could be cured with healing.

After the first two sessions the pain disappeared, and he was delighted. But as he was about to leave my spirit doctor told me that he also had a small benign lump in the groin and that this should be removed medically. Jimmy's face crumpled when I passed this message on. 'I'm not going to any bloody doctor!' he cried. 'The last one I saw nearly killed my mother by giving her the wrong prescription.'

I spent some time reassuring him. 'Look,' I said, 'I would not have been given this message if it would put you in any kind of danger.'

'Why can't your spirit doctors get rid of it?' he asked.

'I have no idea, but I do trust them,' I replied.

I persuaded him to visit his doctor eventually, who was not only surprised by the absence of the hernia but was amazed that Jimmy should be aware of the lump in the groin. It was so small that the doctor could barely locate it himself.

Jimmy had the lump removed, and it was benign, but the reason why it was necessary for him to have it removed medically and not spiritually became obvious when he was found to be in the first stages of diabetes.

I received another diagnosis for Irene, a woman in her late forties.

She had asked for healing for severe headaches. During the healing I was told that she had an aneurysm and that she needed immediate surgery and intensive healing after the event.

I was in a dilemma. I felt that I could not give her the diagnosis, but did suggest that she should see a specialist. She took my advice and after many tests my diagnosis was confirmed.

She came to see me two months later, and during that healing session a voice told me that Irene was going to be alright now. I passed this message on, and she laughed.

'I believe them!' she said. 'They have saved my life.' But she did tell me later that, although she had recovered, she had been convinced that the same thing was going to happen again. I am pleased to say that she was wrong, and my informant was right. I was to see her many times in the following years for her 'top-up', as she used to call it, and she never suffered from headaches again.

There were times, however, when the spirit doctors were adamant that my patient should not receive medical treatment. One such person was Peggy.

She had been overcome by the power of the healing energies, and had gone into a deep sleep whilst having treatment. My hands were placed lightly on her stomach when I felt a presence behind me and a hand pressing on my shoulder. Then a voice said, 'Tell her the operation will not be necessary.' Peggy had told me that she had been advised to have a hysterectomy as she had fibroids in the womb. The voice continued, 'Take your hands away.' As I removed my hands they were replaced by a spinning vortex of energy which remained for approximately five minutes.

While this was taking place I heard whispering in the corner of the room. I could not see anyone, but the whispering continued for several minutes. During this time I felt as though I was levitating, although my feet were planted firmly on the floor. When I had finished healing I left to answer the telephone, and when I returned the room was filled with a haze of blue energy.

Peggy was awake now.

'I've been to the most beautiful place!' she told me. 'The colours were out of this world.'

I laughed, and told her that she had indeed been out of this world. I then gave her the whole story. She was thrilled, and delighted that she would not have to go through the trauma of an operation. But before she left I advised her to visit her gynaecologist for a check-up.

I had a telephone call from her the following week. She was shrieking with laughter.

'Betty,' she said, 'you should have seen his face when he told me there was no trace of any fibroids. I told him about the healing and he just shrugged his shoulders and said, "I've never believed in healing, but with this evidence I may just change my mind." But he added, "Don't quote me on it."'

I wondered how many years it would take for the medical profession to accept that there were many healing alternatives where drugs and surgery could be avoided. One of the simplest is a healthy diet and the identification of vitamin and mineral deficiencies.

A young lady in her twenties visited me for healing. Jane was suffering from asthma, eczema and numerous fleeting aches and pains.

She had been having treatment from her GP for two years, until she had insisted that he refer her to the local hospital for a complete check. They had given her the usual drugs and ointment, but nothing had worked. She was in despair. Then a friend told her about healing. She made an appointment to come and see me.

While I was healing her, I noticed a white energy building up at the end of the couch. As always when this happened I felt excited, and my whole body was tingling. Then Jane sat up.

'My God!' she exclaimed. 'I feel as though I've been plugged into an electric socket.'

I persuaded her to lie down again, and explained what was happening. It can sometimes be a little frightening if one is not used to healing energies. Unlike Peggy, Jane was being stimulated so much that she never stopped asking questions and I had to ask her to be quiet for awhile. During the silence I heard a voice say, very distinctly, 'The cat has to go.' I asked Jane whether she had a cat, if so, how old it was. She told me that Poppy was just over two and the love of her life. Then she frowned, and said, 'How did you know that I have a cat?' I passed on the message, and informed her that she was apparently allergic to cats. Jane burst into tears.

'I can't possibly get rid of her, I love her too much,' she said. When she eventually stopped crying we both sat quietly, working out the timing. It was obvious that her allergies had begun when she had acquired Poppy. It became clear to us both that her pet was the problem. Before she left, Jane asked me to continue with the healing, hoping that it would cure her allergies, and avoid a painful parting from her pet. Two months passed and, although she was a bit better, we both realized that the message I received had been correct.

I decided to meditate and to ask for a solution to the problem. It is a practice I have always used for my own problems, and I am constantly surprised by the unusual methods that are used to solve them. This was to be no exception. An acquaintance of Jane's was heartbroken when her own cat had died of old age, and having learned through the grapevine of Jane's predicament, begged her to let her have Poppy. Jane eventually let her beloved pet go, knowing that she would be well looked after. Three weeks later, with further healing, the asthma, eczema and the aches and pains had vanished.

A word of warning though, to anyone suffering from the same complaints. Please do not blame your animal. Every case is different, and there are a hundreds of reasons why people suffer with these disturbing ailments. Stress is the main factor, and, of course, we can have an allergic reaction to humans too. So please, love and care for your animals. They too have the potential to heal.

I have given a detailed description in *Mind Waves* about how I was taught to give psychic surgery on the energy counterpart, but the whole story would be a book in itself. During the training period, I became aware of a particularly powerful personality working with me. I think he must have been attracted by my enthusiasm, because when he was around the atmosphere was electric. He pushed me to the limits, and it was this man who was mainly responsible for the eventual fine-tuning of my mediumship. Sometimes the diagnosis he gave me was complicated, and I could feel his irritation when I questioned it. Otherwise, we had a perfect partnership. Once, when I asked his name, he told me that names are of no consequence. It is the quality of the personality that is important. We *did* think alike. He also told me that continually thinking in terms of 'self' puts the mind into a vacuum which makes it impossible for us to link up with the Universal Mind and the source of all knowledge. In other words, egotists will find themselves perpetually static, unable to think of new ideas or find alternative paths.

I had occasion to doubt a diagnosis many times, and once argued my case quite forcibly. My patient was a man in his fifties, suffering from a persistent backache which prevented him from following his occupation as a builder. A medical specialist had diagnosed a slipped disc and I could see from the energy patterns that this was correct. The diagnosis given by my spirit doctor was a complete energy blockage in the groin. I could not see this, and so I questioned his opinion. This sparked off a few mental fireworks, which I felt were unjustified at the time. I would have eased the energy from the top of the head, to alleviate pressure on the spine and enable the disc to slip back into position. However, as the operation progressed I could see clearly that my teacher was right and that I had been presumptuous, as most students are. He removed a dark tight ball from deep inside the groin area, and informed me that it was a longstanding energy blockage. Immediately I could see energy rushing around the body like a miniature waterfall. My tutor then said, 'That's it,' and left. He had not touched the back at all.

My patient was over the moon when he found the pain had gone. He strutted around the room, bent backwards and forwards, and laughed with delight as he became aware that his slipped disc had been cured.

Because the man had been quite sceptical about healing, and had only agreed to visit me to keep his wife happy, I did not tell him the true story. I did tell his wife later though, and she passed the information on to her husband.

'I don't give a damn who did it,' he said. 'I think healing is bloody marvellous.'

You might well ask, after reading the chapters so far, whether I am really living on this planet. And believe me, I asked myself the same question, over and over again during this period. Although I had always been a very spiritual person, my feet were very firmly on the ground, and yet my day-to-day life had been turned upside down. My previously very private home had been turned into a healing sanctuary, and the telephone never stopped ringing.

For as long as I can remember I had always been a seeker of knowledge, and perhaps this is the key to the mystery. Always looking outward instead of inward, I was projecting my mind energy into space, where it could absorb information from the Universal Mind. At the time I knew nothing of mind energy, but I was obviously doing the right thing, because my psychic powers had been developing all the time.

I had also been captivated by the information one could extract from the hand, and I practised palmistry and, later, medical hand analysis. Again, the focus on the hand became almost meditational and my mind, during these sessions, was free and expansive.

When I was in my early twenties – more than forty years ago – I studied vitamin and mineral therapy. Information was scarce then, but I was able to obtain the white papers, listing all the latest discoveries, from the famous Mayo Clinic in New York. They were way ahead of their time, and so was I. When I saw the transformation they brought to my own young family, and actually cured the dermatitis that my husband had suffered from since the war, I spent the rest of my life recommending remedies to anyone who would listen. I suppose there were those who might have considered me to be a crank but, to be honest, I never thought about it. I was too busy learning.

I had been similarly absorbed by my singing career, and had spent most of my time listening to and studying opera.

Opera, hand analysis, and vitamin and mineral therapy. In retrospect, I realize that I have always chosen to follow subjects that are open to ridicule. Was this chance, or was it planned from another dimension? After all, I had seen and heard spirits from a very young age. Why then, had I not been remotely interested in spiritualism – especially as my paternal grandmother had been a medium and spiritualist. I do not know! Neither do I know why the subject of the paranormal never crossed my mind. As far as I was concerned, the hand analysis was scientific.

I now believe that it was all part of a great plan. As the medium remarked when I first visited him, 'You have been reading hands for so long did you not realize that you were healing people whilst holding their hands.' At the time, as you might have read in *Mind to Mind*, I thought he was crazy to suggest such a thing.

Over the years, vitamin and mineral therapy has saved my life more than once, and it has also helped hundreds of others who took my advice.

The singing! Well, it taught me discipline. And my wonderful singing teacher taught me how to listen, which is the most important part of mediumship, for listening in this profession becomes as much of an art form as it does with singing. A favourite phrase of mine is 'listening to the audible silence'. Once you have found the key to another dimension, it is amazing to hear just how much 'hubble and bubble' is going on. It is rather like listening to the muted whispers of an audience before the conductor appears on the rostrum. There were so many conductors in my life at this stage but, when they raised the baton, peace reigned and there was a pure clarity in the voices of the communicators.

One such person told me something very important.

The planet in which you live is only a small cog in a gigantic wheel. But it is an important cog because the dimensions are indivisible, and negative influences have a devastating effect on the whole. Remember, the visible is only a minute part of the invisible.

Even though you may not be aware of the reason for our visits, not one single word or one particle of energy is ever wasted. It has all been measured.

Mind blowing words indeed. I have never forgotten them.

CHAPTER FOUR

I WAS HEALING A YOUNG BOY ONE DAY, when a spirit communicator indicated that he wanted to work through me. No name was given, but the power of his personality engulfed me, and I felt as though I was in a dreamlike state, as if I was floating. He then told me to repeat what he said, and although I did not actually hear him speaking again, the words that came from my mouth were certainly not mine.

'I want you to close your eyes and listen to my voice,' I told the boy. 'You will feel your body becoming heavier and heavier, and as it does so your problem will disappear. You will feel happy and peaceful. Relax.

'You are now in a complete state of relaxation. Your body will feel light and you will be relieved of the pressure this affliction has caused. Remember, you have no problems.

'You are getting lighter and lighter, lighter and lighter. You may now open your eyes.'

When the child opened his eyes I was amazed at the difference in him. His eyes were actually sparkling, as though they had been lit from behind – very different indeed to the young boy who had entered my healing room with such trepidation. When he sat up, his eyes travelled around the room and I could see that he was having difficulty in trying to relocate himself.

'I have been to heaven!' he told me. He was very excited, and described his journey into another dimension. 'It was so bright and full of wonderful colours and I saw a lot of people. But they didn't wear the same clothes as we do, they wore long white dresses.' He laughed. 'Even the men wore dresses.' He was still talking animatedly to his mother as they left.

As it happened, my next patient was also a young boy who came in with his mother. I was given the same instructions and as I followed them he fell asleep. When he awoke, he told us of the very special place that he had visited, and of the wonderful colours, birds and animals.

I had so many appointments that there was no time to wonder about this new talent, but my healing room seemed to be electrically charged for the rest of the day.

Later, when I had a chance to think about this new episode, I marvelled at what had happened to me whilst I was actually giving hypnotherapy. For that is what it was. My mind had also partially left my body, and not only could I see my spirit teacher but I could also clearly see the energy counterpart of the patient – which confirmed that one does not see with the eyes but with the mind. The mind is made up of the same elements as the other dimension, and when it expands it becomes our 'third eye'.

It was quite extraordinary how this new encounter changed my life yet again. Whenever I practised hypnotherapy the atmosphere became so charged that I received a shock whenever I touched anything metal. It was also obvious to my patients that something remarkable was happening as the following stories indicate.

An elderly gentleman had been visiting me for three weeks. He had chronic arthritis, and although I had been able to alleviate his physical pain, his mental agony over the way he had treated his late wife was still intense – so much so that he confided to me that he did not want to live. On his fourth visit I became aware of the awesome presence of my spirit teacher. As always, the atmosphere in the room was electric. My patient seemed to have gone into a deep sleep without my having uttered a word, and almost against my own will I went through the hypnotic routine. It seemed rather odd at the time, as the man was obviously already relaxed. Then my teacher said, 'All will be well.' He was certainly a man of few words, and I wondered whether his power over others had prevented him from becoming a good conversationalist. *He* certainly had not been a politician, of that I am sure!

I brought my patient out of his trance and gave him a few minutes to pull himself together. His first words were, 'I saw her, I saw my wife!' Although he was smiling, the tears were pouring down his face and soaking into his shirt. He sat up and, still looking dazed, told me that he had been in a room that had had a bright orange glow, and whilst he was gazing around, a door opened and his wife walked in.

'She told me that I must stop worrying,' he said, 'and that there had been faults on both sides.' He held my hand as he slowly dried his tears. 'She told me that she still loved me, you know.' Twisting his handkerchief in his hands, he said, 'I don't know how she can, I'm such a miserable old bugger.' I told him that I had not met one perfect person in my life and was never likely to, and this seemed to cheer him up. He asked me how it was that he could see his wife, even though she was dead. I told him of the phenomenon of mind energy, and explained how the presence that had entered the room had done so with a specific aim in mind – to expand his mind energy to such an extent that he could see into the other dimension. Like so many other healings, the meeting with his wife had obviously been arranged before his visit to me.

Although his arthritis had gone, my patient visited me every week for the next five weeks, hoping that he would relive the experience. But it was not to be. I taught him the rudiments of telepathy, and assured him that he could talk to his wife at any time and that she would be able to hear him.

Six months later, I received a card from India. He was there studying Buddhism. A seed had been sown, and he was obviously reaping the harvest.

My next story is about a young man named Martin.

When Martin first visited me he was suffering with acne, pains in his arms and legs, frequent headaches and a host of other minor ailments.

I gave him healing on three separate occasions, but it became obvious to both of us that the healing simply was not working. Because of the success I was having with healing in general, I was surprised and disappointed and so, of course, was Martin.

However, I persuaded him to return for a fourth visit. As he walked into the room he looked around and said, 'Have you been burning incense or something?'

'No! Why do you ask?'

'Well, the room is full of blue smoke,' he told me.

'Can you smell anything?' I enquired.

'Well no, I can't.' He frowned, and said, 'What is it?'

I explained that it was healing energy, and that very often it was so dense that people could not see me, and thought I had vanished.

'There is so much power in the room I think something great is going to happen,' I told him. Before I had finished the sentence I could feel the power of my hypnotherapy teacher moving in, and so could Martin.

'Betty, I think there is a spirit here, I can feel it.' As he spoke, his eyes were alight with wonder. 'I've never seen a spirit,' he said.

I slowly talked him into a hypnotic state and, as I did so, I could feel my own mind energy lifting and the now familiar floating feeling. I looked at Martin's body and saw a map of the meridian lines and chakras. But the most amazing sight was the mind energy – it was so compressed that it became obvious to me why the hands on healing had not worked. I remember thinking that it would take a miracle to disperse the congestion. And the miracle was about to happen. I watched silently as fingers of mind energy started to leave my patient's head, slowly at first and then with a rush. The fingers of energy turned into a cloud, and gradually formed the normal shape of a halo around his head. Looking again at the meridian lines and vortices, I was delighted to see the activity that was taking place in the energy counterpart. It was all systems go!

Just as I was about to talk Martin out of his relaxed state I happened to look up and there before me was my spirit tutor. Unfortunately, I was unable to take in his appearance because on eye contact I was quite simply, knocked out. I opened my eyes when I felt someone shaking me. It was Martin.

'Were you in a trance?' he asked.

'I think I must have been,' I replied.

'I think I have been too,' he said. 'I saw this man standing beside me, and he was talking to me.'

'What did he say?' I asked.

'He was telling me to wake up, but I didn't want to, and then he put his hand on me. It gave me such a shock that I woke up, and then I saw you sitting there in a kind of trance.' He was smiling. 'I don't know what you've done to me but I feel great.' He was jumping up and down now, and swinging his arms around. 'I can't feel a thing, the pain has gone.'

He was fascinated when I explained what had been happening. I was about to question him about his life, because I did not want him to get into such a bad state again, when a woman's voice came through.

'I'm his granny,' she said. 'He won't tell you, but he makes himself ill because he can't read.' I passed this message on. Martin's face was bright red, and he sat with his head in his hands for some time before he spoke.

'I'm mortified when people find out that I can't read.' he said, then sat up. 'What else does she say?'

His granny then gave him the most wonderful survival evidence. When she had finished, he told me that this had been the most incredible day of his life.

'Are you going to do something about this problem?' I asked. 'You simply cannot go through life not being able to read.'

'What can I do?' he replied. 'I would look a right mug trying to go back to school at my age.'

'Would you go to a private teacher if I could find one for you?' I asked.

'Yes, but I'm dyslexic, I don't think anyone can help.'

I was able to find a teacher for him and, after testing him, she found that he was not dyslexic. The teacher in question could not understand why he had never been able to learn to read, as he was such an excellent pupil. Within a year he was reading and writing with ease and had also found himself an interesting clerical position with a large electronics firm. With effort, he had completely turned his life around.

I believe the mind energy blockage had been pressing on his brain for many years, hence his inability to learn.

During this time I offered hypnotherapy to many people with severe physical problems, and those who were adventurous enough to have faith were certainly rewarded.

When I was alone, I speculated as to who the entity was who performed so powerfully during these sessions. It was during one of these meditative moods that I was given a vision of a white cloud with a vortex in the centre and as it spun, a group of spirit entities emerged, giving the impression that they were descending an unseen ladder. Then the vision faded and another took its place. Dozens of these vortices were hovering over a vast stretch of land, and blue energy was streaming out of them. It swirled around, covering the whole scene and was finally drawn back into the vortices. For many months I was to wonder about these visions and their meaning, and I finally came to the conclusion that I was being shown how spirit entities can enter this dimension for a while, but have to return when the blue energy is drawn back into the vortices. This was corroborated one day when I was giving healing.

I had my hands on a patient's head when I saw a spirit doctor standing opposite me. As I looked at him, the room filled with a blue healing energy. Towards the end of the treatment I heard him say, 'It is time for me to go.' Immediately, the blue energy in the room began to swirl and the spirit doctor disappeared into a vortex. I could feel the power evaporate and assumed that the healing had been successful.

I believe that these vortices are the doors to the energy dimension, and when we meditate we may occasionally spin through them, allowing us to have a glimpse of the magical world of the afterlife.

This brought me back to the question of the spirit hypnotherapist. Why was he so much more powerful than the other doctors who worked through me? What was his secret? I was to find out about two weeks later.

Lynne, a young married woman with two children, was having terrible nightmares. She came to me in desperation, as she had not had a good night's sleep for about a year and had become so weary that she could not look after her family. I gave her hypnotherapy and immediately felt the presence of my spirit friend, only this time it was different. At first it was as though our two minds were one, then the power of his mind overshadowed mine and I became such a powerful personality that I felt as though I could change the world. I sensed I had a knowledge that was unique, and I realized that it was this person's knowledge that gave him power.

It was through this evidence that I recognized the importance of seeking knowledge, and how this in turn strengthens the mind. I also understand how powerful minds are attracted by like minds, and under certain circumstances can overpower the mind of the medium and put them into a trance state. Which was to be the next step of my mediumship.

CHAPTER FIVE

I WAS ENJOYING A RELAXED, cosy chat with a friend one after-noon, when I felt a presence behind me. I was not at all pleased, as this was supposed to be my day off. I told my friend about the presence.

'If you don't accept that it is there,' she said, 'it will go away.'

Unfortunately, it did not. I could feel the pressure as it came closer, and could feel my facial muscles being pulled around; I had no control over them at all. The last thing I remember was being overwhelmed by a feeling of lethargy, and a total inability to communicate. I awoke to find my friend staring at me.

'Are you okay?' she asked, her eyes anxiously scanning my face. 'Betty, you turned into a Chinaman!'

'You must be joking,' I replied.

'No, really!' she exclaimed. 'Your features changed completely, even the shape of your eyes.' Still looking at me intently, she said, 'Surely you must know what happened to you?' When I told her that I couldn't remember anything, she said that a man with a Chinese accent had spoken to her, through me, giving her survival evidence from a friend, who had died two years previously. She was so happy that I was delighted for her, but as I had no recollection I was some-what concerned by this new and unwanted talent.

I did not mind the doctors helping me whilst I was healing because, most of the time, I was in control. But to have someone else taking over completely was not something I appreciated. Trying to make sense of this phenomenon, I asked my friend to describe the transfor-mation.

'At first,' she said, 'I noticed a change in your features, but it was so fleeting that I convinced myself it was my imagination. Your head sank onto your chest for a few minutes, then you sat upright, and your face had changed into that of a Chinaman. I was shocked at first, but when he spoke, his voice was so compassionate that I lost all fear.'

When I asked her to describe the voice she told me that the man had had a very noticeable Chinese accent, and had even spoken a few words in Chinese.

My friend was still overwhelmed by her experience and said repeatedly that she couldn't believe it had happened to her. She told me that she thought she would have been frightened to death, but instead had found it absolutely fascinating. Then she paused, and said, 'You never knew my friend Clara, did you? She died before we met, which is even more convincing.'

We talked for about an hour, and she told me that when the evidence had come to an end my head had dropped again, as before, and when I straightened up my face had returned to normal.

I was absolutely stunned. Over the past three years I felt I had dealt stoically with everything that had happened to me, but this was different, I had not been in control. I did not like that at all.

I asked my friend to keep this episode confidential. I felt that I had enough to deal with without this becoming common knowledge, and I suppose, in a way, that I was ashamed at having allowed someone to take me over to that extent. I saw it as a sign of weakness. Later, for some unknown reason, I made an appointment to have a sitting with a well-known London medium. I had no idea why I chose her or, to be truthful, why I was going in the first place.

We sat quietly for a few moments and then she said, 'I have a Chinaman coming through, and he is saying that it is he who taught you about the meridian lines and chakras. That he has been helping you to understand the elements of life-force and how it works. Now you are on your own.' The medium looked at me, and said, 'What on earth is he talking about? Meridian lines and chakras? I've never heard of them!'

I had to hide my smile, because it was obvious that she was completely out of her depth. But the message was more convincing for that reason, and the pleasure it brought me was immense, as the realization dawned that when my tutor had taken me over it was to say goodbye. I found this very touching. I never felt his presence again, but I hope he received my message of thanks, for without his tuition my diagnoses would not have been so successful.

I had another reason to be grateful to him. He had shown me that we do have a consciousness outside of the physical body, and that it was possible for one mind to overshadow another. The evidence in support of the mind energy factor was immense, and I longed to share my experiences with the world. But I knew that I had to wait until my theories were foolproof.

On another occasion, my daughter Janet and I were invited to sit with a group of people to meditate and give absent healing. Again, I felt the pressure of a presence as it stood behind me, and then the familiar lethargy and facial contortions. This time, it was was a Norwegian doctor. When I awoke, the group was discussing the evidence that the doctor had given them, but one look at Janet's face told me that she was furious. The group told me that the doctor had given them a spiritual lecture, before turning to one person in particular to offer advice, which was sorely needed at that time. They were even more impressed when they found that he had left an apport, a spirit offering, in my lap. It was not a valuable item, but it was a very unusual stone.

On our way home Janet said, 'Don't you ever do that to me again, it was horrible.'

I tried to tell her that I had no control over the situation, but she argued that I could have stopped it happening if I had so wished. 'You frightened me to death. Don't ever ask me to go anywhere with you again.'

Janet was only in her teens at this time, and through my own experiences had been thrown in at the deep end. Her reaction troubled me. Was I asking too much of my family to back me in my pursuit of mediumship and healing? After all, our family home had been turned into a sanctuary for others, with people coming and going all the time and the telephone ringing continually. I decided to have a family conference, and the outcome was that they agreed to back me all the way.

The strange thing was that, unbeknown to any of us, Janet was herself in the first stages of becoming a medium. When this eventually grew obvious, she made it quite clear that she had no intention of involving herself with the paranormal. But, like her mother before her, she gradually became involved through her work as a yoga teacher. Later, as an experienced medium, she was to find out that when a powerful personality takes over there is very little one can do about it.

There have been many times when she has been speaking on the telephone with a friend that Janet has taken on the features and speech of a relative when giving survival evidence.

Whilst giving healing I have been entranced by many personalities. One of these was a young girl of about sixteen years of age. Several people told me that I looked very young when healing, but it was an artist who gave me the most detailed description of this young person. Apparently, she had fair hair falling over her shoulders, high cheekbones and full lips. I thought she sounded rather familiar, and mentioned this to my artist friend.

'As a matter of fact, she looks rather like you,' he said, 'but that may be because her face manifests over your own.' We were both intrigued, and wondered who this young lady could be. And why should a person as young as that entrance me whilst healing? My friend's wife was so curious when he told her about this episode that she phoned immediately to make an appointment for herself. I explained that it was not a regular happening, and that the young girl had only been seen by a dozen people at the most, but she still insisted on visiting me.

'The healing will do me good, anyway,' she said. When she arrived for her appointment I went straight into my healing mode, as I call it. I immediately felt spaced out, as I always did when a spirit entity was around and then, nothing. It must have been thirty minutes later when I opened my eyes and found my patient looking at me as though she had also been entranced.

'Betty, it was marvellous. This girl is so young, my husband's description was absolutely spot on.' She spoke excitedly for about ten minutes.

'What I do not understand,' I said, 'is why a girl as young as that should be here whilst I am healing. Surely, she can't have the experience needed to help in the healing process.'

'Well, the room was positively vibrating whilst she was here, so she must have a lot of power of some kind,' she replied.

It was a complete mystery to me, and as there is no memory recall when one is taken over by an entity I had to rely on the information given to me. I did not mention this young lady to anyone else, so each person thought their observation was unique. And as those who saw her were not known to each other – apart from the artist and his wife – the information could not have been passed on. I also asked each individual a specific question about the young lady's appearance and I was satisfied, in every case, that they had actually seen her.

She was to appear intermittently over the next twelve years, until I had lunch with the medium who had first forecast my mediumship and healing career. We had not met for many years. We chatted during our lunch, and when we reached the coffee stage, he suddenly said, 'I have a young girl here,' and went on to describe the young lady. 'She is telling me that she is your daughter. Have you lost a child?'

'No, I haven't,' I replied, shaken by his words.

'Well, my dear,' he said, 'we must get to the bottom of this.'

He sat with his eyes closed, and then he said, 'She is telling me that she was one of two, twins in fact.'

I was completely stunned by this information, as I had, in fact, miscarried twins at three months, much too early to have known what sex they were. When I told him this he simply said, 'Well, there you are then. I knew I couldn't be wrong because I could see and hear her so clearly.'

'Will you ask her if she has been with me for some time?' I said.

'I don't have to ask her,' he replied. 'I know she has. She has just told me.'

Once my daughter had identified herself, she was not seen again. I only wish that I had been able to see her but, so far, this has never happened.

I hope this story will give help to those who have grieved over losing babies in the early months of pregnancy. Even though the babies have moved on into another dimension, they still regard themselves as our children. They chose us in the first place, after all, and one day we will all meet again.

It is amazing how, when one mind overshadows another, the features change. Sometimes it is only gestures, but they are immediately recognized by the person receiving the survival evidence. It may be that I brush my hair back from my face, not a habit of mine, and I am told that it is identical to the gesture used by the communicator when they were alive. It can be a touch, a look, a mannerism, or an irritating habit, but there will be no doubt on the part of the sitter that it is someone whom they have known, even if they have not identified themselves.

In my book *Mind Waves* I told the story of how one very sceptical man saw my features change into that of a Red Indian, my blonde hair disappearing under a mane of long black hair. Michael Bentine also saw the same transfiguration when I was giving him healing. It did not bother Michael at all as he has been involved with the paranormal since he was a child, but it can be a shock if one is simply sitting in on a treatment.

In 1977, as I moved into my fourth year as a medium and healer, this process was all still a mystery to me, but it later became obvious that the brain is the computer and the mind the power that motivates it. Without the power, the brain is dead. Therefore, when another mind moves in and takes over, the input from that mind transfers itself to the brain, and the physical body will then take on the features and mannerisms of that person. The mind also holds the records of past and present lives, and from it we can extract past talents and make them work for us in this life.

The whole thing turned around on me when I visited another

medium in London. We did not know each other at the time, so, after a brief handshake, I sat down with her. Immediately, I saw her head drop to her chest; when she sat up straight her face had changed and she spoke to me in a deep, masculine voice. She was in trance. I was given the most wonderful survival evidence and advice. When she returned to normal I thanked her, and she said, 'You must be very powerful. I would normally need the help of several friends before going into trance.' I asked her the reason for this.

'Well, you see, my dear, the spirits have to draw their strength from us to be able to stay here.' I was learning all the time. As I was about to leave, she placed her hand on my shoulder, and said, 'You have a beautiful soul.' It was the nicest thing that anyone had ever said to me; in times of despair, I have often thought about that statement, and it has given me hope.

If only people would look at the whole concept scientifically then they would find it easier to understand, and most of their unnecessary fear would diminish.

I am often asked if I was ever frightened in those early years.

The answer is yes, and when you read the following chapter you will understand my momentary fears. But the fear soon evaporated when I felt the protective presence of my spirit friends.

CHAPTER SIX

I WAS GIVING HEALING TO A WOMAN in her fifties when I saw that she was being overshadowed by an unpleasant spirit entity. She began to cry.

'I feel dreadful,' she said. I tried to calm her, but to no avail. Then I heard a voice saying, 'I will never leave her, she is mine.' The voice sounded so vindictive that I became afraid of the intruder, but knew instinctively what I had to do. I began by silently repeating the Lord's Prayer, an action that had helped to calm me in the early days. As I did so, I saw the entity surrounded by a bright white light, and at this point I could see that it was a man. He began to scream, and the woman put her hands over her ears. I felt a protective wall of energy form around me, then I asked the entity to leave and told him that he would be looked after and could eventually be happy. I visualized him surrounded by blue healing energy, but he still tried to hang onto the woman. I had the impression, from the angle of his spirit body, that someone was trying to pull him away, and that was why he was screaming. I was still asking him to leave peacefully – though I had nearly given up – when he disappeared.

Although I was feeling decidedly shaky, my first thought was to calm the woman, and as I did so, she told me a remarkable story.

When she was twenty, she had married a man ten years older than herself. He had persuaded her to leave England and emigrate to South Africa, to settle down in the outback. Although she had a beautiful home and servants, she was very unhappy, for as the months went by she realized that not only was her husband a sadist, but he also enjoyed sexual parties where everyone paired off with someone else's partner.

'Car keys were left on a table when the guests arrived,' she told me. 'Then when everyone was in an alcoholic stupor at the end of the evening, the ladies picked up the keys and went off into the night with the owner.' She absolutely refused to have anything to do with this practice.

Her life became increasingly miserable, and finally, aided by a man friend, she returned to England. Unfortunately, no matter where she went her husband tracked her down, and because of this she had two nervous breakdowns. Although she had remarried it seemed that nothing could be done to stop him pestering her, until one fateful day he had a heart attack on her doorstep and died.

'I know this might sound dreadful,' she said, 'but I was glad he was dead, and he couldn't abuse me any more.' She put her hands over her face, and continued, 'I was wrong. He's been haunting me ever since. I have even seen him. It's horrible.'

At this point I described what had happened during the healing session and asked her whether she had been aware that something unusual was going on.

'No!' she answered. 'I just felt terrible, and thought it was because of the healing.'

'But you put your hands over your ears when he screamed,' I said, 'I assumed that you had heard him.'

'I can't tell you why I did that,' she replied. 'Perhaps my body felt the vibration.'

I suggested that she should have further healing, and made an appointment for her to visit me the following week.

This had been my first experience of exorcism and I felt totally shattered. I believe I was being guided when I said the Lord's Prayer, and by subsequent actions that I took. They were entirely spontaneous, so someone must have been with me, helping me.

I was understandably rather nervous when her next appointment was due. However, I was pleasantly surprised when, on opening the door, I came face to face with a totally different human being. Her face was radiant, and she pushed a huge bouquet of flowers into my arms.

'He's gone, Betty,' she shouted. 'The bastard has gone!' I put my arms around her and we walked into the healing room.

'I don't think I need healing any more,' she said, 'but perhaps you should lay your hands on me for luck.' She went on to tell me that the black cloud she had always felt around her had gone, and for the first time in thirty years she felt that she had a wonderful life ahead.

Before she left I warned her not to think of her husband ever again as this would encourage him to return. 'Don't worry,' she replied. 'I will never do anything to encourage him to return.'

A year later she bought a villa in Portugal. We kept in touch and I was delighted to hear, years later, that she was still very happy in her second marriage.

The next exorcism took place when I visited an old inn with a friend.

We were sitting having a quiet drink when I noticed that the bartender was being overshadowed by an entity. It is an entirely different sensation than that experienced when one sees an ordinary apparition. There is a sense, and even a smell of evil. At first, I tried to ignore it, but decided to tell my friend about it when he noticed my interest in the barman. We spent a few minutes discussing the situation.

'If the man is in trouble and you can help,' he said, 'perhaps you should.'

I laughed. 'What am I supposed to say? "Hallo! Did you know that you have an undesirable spirit around you?" I don't think he'd be very pleased.'

'Well, can't you do it quietly' he suggested. 'Does he have to know?'

'I suppose not,' I replied, then I closed my eyes and silently recited the Lord's Prayer, asking that the intruder be banished. Once again, I saw the bright light around the entity. Eventually, I saw it being pulled away from the man, and he was free.

Some time later we heard this man's story. We were having a

relaxed break in the same pub when my friend entered into a conversation with the barman. He told my companion that he had been a heavy drinker but on pouring himself a drink one night he found that he had lost the desire to drink, so he poured it away and had not indulged since.

'It was really odd,' he said, 'because as a rule I couldn't wait for the first sip of the night.'

'How long ago was this?' my friend asked.

The barman thought for a moment, then he said, 'It was about three months ago.' When my friend joined me and repeated the conversation I looked at my diary. It was exactly three months since we had last visited the inn.

I was to find out much later that alcoholics who pass into the next dimension often attach themselves to other drinkers so that they can still enjoy the sensation.

Although effecting an exorcism can be a blessed relief for the person concerned, the aftermath for me was traumatic. When I was alone again I could feel my whole body trembling, and I felt as though I had lost every ounce of energy. I could not sleep, and could only digest liquids. I prayed that it would never happen again – but of course it did. Someone, somewhere, was determined to teach me every aspect of mediumship. Although I was glad of the help from spiritual advisors and spirit doctors, I still did not want this particular gift. I would have been extremely happy just being a healer. While I was in this mood I received a particularly helpful message from my guru.

'In the dimension in which you live,' he told me, 'one has to deal with unpleasant situations. Sometimes the appearance of uninvited guests can be irritating, especially if you do not admire them. But usually, with a lot of charm and even more insistence, we can send them on their way in the hope that they can, in retrospect, understand your actions. If a visitor is charming and a joy to be with, then we welcome them with open arms, invite them in and delight in the conversation.

'The same applies when you see the deterioration of someone's health, affected by the actions of another. A protective barrier is created around that person until a solution is found, or, preferably, the negative personality is removed.

'What you are experiencing is everyday life in the spiritual dimension that mirrors your own. That is all.

'All unpleasant people thrive on attention. If a person is affected by an unwanted visitor then they should totally ignore their existence, and turn their minds to matters of a spiritual nature. Recognizing negative influences weakens the life force and makes one vulnerable. This must never be allowed to happen.'

As the message came to an end I opened my eyes and there, in the corner of the room, was a bright white light, rather like a large illuminated snowball. It hovered for a moment, and then simply melted away. A warmth enveloped me, as though I had been wrapped in a cosy blanket, and as my eyes closed, I remember thinking how natural and simple it all seemed once it had been explained.

The following day I felt rejuvenated and, with the knowledge that one could, quite simply, show unpleasant spirits the door, I looked forward to greeting the first patient of the day.

There were times when the negative spirit had no form, but enveloped the unfortunate victim in a black cloud. In these cases my usual ritual worked, but on the occasions when it did not work, I added a postscript. The following story was one such case.

The patient was a woman named Marjorie, who was in her fifties. She had suffered the most dreadful depression for several years and had tried psychiatrists, drugs, and most of the alternative therapies, all to no avail. I asked her why she thought healing would work.

'Someone told me that you could see the aura,' she said, 'and I wondered if you could see what I can feel.'

'What can you feel?' I asked.

'Well' she replied, 'I know this may sound as if I'm quite barmy, but I think someone is trying to get into my mind.'

I suggested that she lie down on the couch so that I could proceed with the healing. The moment I touched her, a black cloud appeared and covered the upper half of her body, and I knew then that I had to perform an exorcism. However, thirty minutes later, it became obvious that it was not going to work. I looked at my patient. She appeared to be in a deep sleep and it was then that I remembered the message I had received from my guru. Negative spirits dislike being ignored and to get rid of them one should turn to spiritual matters. So I told the entity that he or she was so pathetic that I was not going to waste any more of my valuable time on them – and that I was going to strengthen Marjorie's mind so she would be strong enough to ignore them. The cloud swirled around as though showing anger.

'Wherever you look you will only see light,' I continued. 'This light will overshadow you and will eventually conquer you.' I repeated this over and over, using my hypnotherapy technique. I had no idea whether it was going to work but, at the time, I felt so powerful that I thought it might. Then I closed my eyes and continued with the healing.

About fifteen minutes later Marjorie sat bolt upright and said, 'Crikey! You've just given me an electric shock.' I looked at her and, to my surprise, the black cloud had vanished. I decided that it would not be in Marjorie's best interest to tell her the full story. But I did ask her whether she had ever been obsessed by an image of someone, and she admitted feeling terrible hatred for her late husband when she had found out that he had been having an affair for ten years before he died. I urged her to forget him as it would only draw him nearer to her. She promised that she would try. Later, she told me that every time she tried to think of him her mind went blank.

'It's almost as though he never existed,' she said. Marjorie made a full recovery.

Unfortunately, not all my attempts at exorcism were successful because some people were as negative as the entity that surrounded them. Nothing I did or said affected either of them, and one could only surmise that they deserved each other. I hesitate to call people evil because I do not think one should judge. I prayed for them, and hoped that someone or something would change them so that the attraction of like to like could be severed.

My clairvoyant vision of energies was fascinating, and had opened up a whole new world to me. In retrospect, I could honestly say that the last four years had been the most exciting time of my life. But one always has to pay a price, and mine was the total loss of privacy. Having always been a very private person, this affected me a great deal. I believe that everyone is entitled to seclusion if they wish, when only trusted friends are invited to share the ups and downs.

This was how I viewed the lives of my clients. The information given to me through survival evidence was sacred to them and for them alone, and I honoured this.

There was, however, one aspect of my mediumship that worried me, and that was the quality of the survival evidence. The majority of the messages I received were mundane, and appeared to have no spiritual value. Although the recipients were delighted with the messages, I nevertheless decided to ask, through meditation, for quality and not quantity. I must have upset someone, for it was to be three months before I received any more survival evidence – although at the time this did not worry me at all. In fact I was grateful, hoping that I could now ignore this side of my psychic life. Alas, it was not to be. But something had changed and when the evidence came through once again, it was of a more spiritual nature. Of course, there were the usual family recollections and small talk which is a normal part of our conversations between this world and the next, but added to this were spiritual truths which gave the recipient something to think about in their solitary moments.

A typical example of this was with a woman named Debbie.

Debbie had been sitting with me for about an hour, listening to her late grandmother talking about family matters, when a spirit voice interrupted the conversation and said, 'Do not turn your back on God.'

Debbie looked startled when I passed on this message. 'Was that my grandmother saying that?' she asked.

'No,' I replied, 'It was a man's voice, but he did not give me his name.'

Looking at me intently, she asked, 'Are you religious?'

'No,' I said. 'I was a confirmed member of the Church of England, but left because of the hypocrisy I encountered. Now I have found a spiritual path I am happy with.'

'I know why I've been given that message,' Debbie told me. 'It's because I have decided to give up going to church.' She hesitated, then continued, 'Some of the people there are not religious at all, they are just do-gooders who love interfering in other people's lives.'

I suggested that as she had received such an important message she should go home and think about it.

When she came to see me again nine months later, she was looking happy and contented. She told me that she had stayed away from her church for some time, but had thought a great deal about the message she had received. Then one night, while she was praying, she knew what she had to do. She spent a fortnight visiting three different churches and liked one of them so much that she decided to become a permanent part of the congregation.

Debbie looked delighted. 'If it hadn't been for that message I would never have visited another church,' she said. 'I have you thank for that.'

This is a typical example of what I mean by quality and not quantity. A lot of thought had been given to those few words, and the outcome had given someone back their faith.

I was to receive thousands of examples of how true spiritual communicators get to the point with just a few simple words, provoking thoughts in the recipient which, in most cases, would lead to a decision that transformed their lives.

CHAPTER SEVEN

So much had happened to me over the past few years that I thought I had reached a stage where nothing would surprise me. I was wrong. A young lady arrived for a sitting one day, and asked whether I would mind if she recorded it. I did not mind at all but warned her that the energies around me usually blocked out the voices. This did not deter her, and she went ahead with the recording. She received survival evidence of an intimate nature relating to her marriage. She was advised by her late mother to 'stop telling lies about her husband' and to have the courage to own up and ask his forgiveness. Needless to say she was furious and accused me of making it all up. I pointed out that she was a total stranger to me so I could not possibly have done that. She was so angry that her hands shook when she replayed the tape. There was nothing on it. When she continued to abuse me, I suggested that she left. I have to say that her presence made me feel uneasy, and I was pleased to see her go.

Six months later I was invited to a party and there, with her husband, was this obnoxious lady. I was shocked when I realized that she was married to an extremely nice ex-patient of mine. I tried to avoid her, but she waylaid me and said, 'You won't tell my husband about my visit to you, will you?' I assured her that all of my work was confidential. She smiled, and said, cynically, 'You are so good.' I knew from the survival evidence I had received, that she had been unfaithful to her husband for many years, but stayed with him so that she could still benefit from the lavish lifestyle he gave her, I also knew that I could never betray a confidence, but fervently hoped that, one day, he would be rid of her.

Emotional relationships are so diverse that one would be well

BETTY SHINE

advised not to stand in judgement, but with healing and mediumship it is very difficult to stand aside when one is deliberately drawn into the fray.

The following story is a typical example.

A young lady had asked me for clairvoyance. She sat looking at me with a rapt expression, as though I was going to pull a rabbit out of a hat. I felt uneasy, and decided to tape the conversation I had with her.

'Why are you doing that?' she asked.

'I usually take recordings whilst healing or giving messages. It is for my library,' I replied.

'Can I have a copy?' she asked.

'Yes, if you wish,' I answered. 'Now if you sit quietly I will try to help.'

I saw immediately that she was heading for trouble, and that it was going to be brought about by her own actions. I advised her to change so that when the time came, it would lessen the impact. She assured me that she was doing nothing untoward and that she had not visited me to hear a lot of nonsense. I decided to end the session. When I listened to the tape later that day, I found that it was completely blank, no interference, nothing! A sign that I should put the matter behind me.

Her husband telephoned that night and told me that his wife was very upset and that I ought to be locked up, or something worse. I could not tell him that she was betraying the trust shown by her boss when he had given her the job of looking after his financial affairs. She was, quite simply 'cooking the books'.

Her husband visited me a year later, to apologize. He told me that she had been found out, and had lost her job. Her employers had decided not to prosecute but the shame had destroyed their marriage and he had asked her to leave. I told him that I had only spent a very short time with his wife, but it had been enough for her to realize that clairvoyants can actually 'see' what was happening, and she hadn't enjoyed the experience.

74

'What did she actually say to you that evening?' I asked.

He sighed, 'She told me that you had accused her of being a thief and also of being unfaithful to me.'

I told him that I had not mentioned anything of the kind, and had only told her that she would be in trouble later, through her own actions. Although I knew perfectly well what I was 'seeing' I did not tell her this because it would have been unethical to do so. I also told him that their marriage was never mentioned.

'How can you bear to do this job?' he asked me. 'Let's face it, people could twist every word you say if they want to make a point.'

He was right. Why should I leave myself open to abuse? I loved the healing. I made the decision not to give any more clairvoyant sittings.

My friends were extremely angry at my having been made a scapegoat and tried to persuade me to carry on as usual and not allow one maladjusted person to affect me in this way. But I was adamant. I argued that I truly did not want this kind of aggravation in my life.

'But you are so good,' cried one friend. 'Just look at the help you have given people.' She indicated the group. 'Us included. You can't give it up.'

'I really am sorry but I have made my decision,' I insisted.

In many ways I had been delighted to find that I was psychic, as this explained why I had felt so vulnerable all my life. It is the sensitivity and fine-tuning of the personality which makes a good medium and healer. Like the diamond, every facet has to be cut and polished before it can sparkle like a star. The process can be painful, and there are times when one is tempted to opt out. For me this was one of those times. If one particular facet was to remain unpolished, so be it. But, like a number of my resolutions, this was not to be.

I was having lunch with an acquaintance one day when I 'saw' a house with water swirling around it. I asked the man sitting oppposite me if he was buying a house.

'Yes, as a matter of fact I'm looking at one at the moment.'

I told him about my clairvoyant vision, and he asked me why I was being given this picture.

'I don't know,' I replied, 'but if you give me a minute I may be able to tell you.'

I sat quietly for a moment, and then I told him that I could see water pouring down a hill through a ravine, and overflowing into a garden.

'That doesn't seem possible,' he said. 'Although there is a hill and a ravine at the back of the house I'm hoping to buy, it is quite a way from the property, although I must admit that the ravine does curve toward it slightly. In any event, I've only ever seen a trickle of water running through to a stream below.'

'Have you ever seen this property in the winter?' I asked.

'No! My wife and I have spent quite a lot of time in the area but not, I hasten to add, on this particular property.' He looked puzzled, 'Are you sure there is a problem?' he asked.

'Absolutely,' I replied, and then suggested that he look into the situation, if only for the sake of my reputation. Then added, 'We've been having some pretty foul weather this winter. Perhaps now is the time to have another look before you make your final decision.'

'Betty,' he said. 'You do realize that you're asking me to go all the way to Wales?'

'I still think you should go and take a look,' I replied.

When he told his wife about my clairvoyance, she agreed that they should check it out.

When they arrived, they were horrified to see the front of the property surrounded by water. The ravine was flooded, and there was a lake in what should have been the garden. When they asked around they were told that this happened once or twice every winter and spring. They decided to opt out of the deal.

They later found a beautiful cottage in Devon, and regularly sent me photographs of the garden. On the back of one they had written, 'None of this would have been possible without your intervention. We would have lost everything.'

I was torn, I really didn't want to give clairvoyance on a regular

Clairvoyance

basis. I preferred to teach others to see clearly for themselves. After much thought I decided that I would only help close friends. It was during one of these sittings that something extraordinary happened.

I was giving clairvoyance to Charlie, a friend of mine. We had been sitting together for about an hour, when we heard clicking noises coming from the tape recorder. Then we felt an icy draught around our feet, accompanied by the sound of whispering. Neither of us spoke during this time, but just looked at each other in amazement. The phenomenon lasted about ten minutes, then it stopped as suddenly as it had begun. I looked at the tape recorder and said, laughingly, 'Do you think they've left us a message?'

'You are joking aren't you?' my friend replied.

'Yes I am, but I'll play it back anyway. You never know.'

As usual there was a lot of interference, and we had great difficulty in hearing the conversation. Then as clear as crystal, a voice said, 'Charlie, Charlie, I love you.' I looked at Charlie, and said, 'It's for you.'

He was dumbstruck, 'That was Elle,' he said, 'I don't believe it, that was Elle.' Tears were streaming down his face.

I smiled at him. 'I know. Nobody could forget her voice.'

Although we listened to the rest of the tape, that was the only message.

'Betty, how did Elle's voice get on the tape? I don't understand,' he said.

'I have no idea,' I replied. 'But it is proof that she has survived.'

'I must confess that I've never believed in life after death, until now.' He sat holding his head in his hands for a moment, then looked up and said, 'I've been feeling guilty about my forthcoming marriage, because I felt I was letting Elle down.'

'Well, I think she has given her approval, otherwise she would not have made the effort to leave the message.'

'Betty, rewind the tape and let's listen to it again,' Charlie asked.

We listened to the tape three times, but the voice of Elle had disappeared. Although we were both disappointed, nothing could take away the joy of having heard her voice once more.

When Charlie had gone I thought about his wife and the terrible shock it had been to us all when we heard of her sudden death. It was now three years since that day.

I was to meet Charlie and his new bride a year later, they were extremely happy. They told me that Elle's photograph had pride of place in their living room and that they spoke to her often.

It was at this time that I read an article about a medium in Germany who had received several spirit voices on tape. I was fascinated, and decided to use the tape recorder more frequently.

Six months later I was giving healing to a man in his forties. Like most of my patients, he fell asleep as soon as I had placed my hands upon him. I woke him when I had finished and asked whether he would like to hear the interference that the energies wrought on the tape. He was very interested, so I began to play it back. At the beginning of the tape was the sound of a man with a terrible hacking cough. My patient turned to me and said, 'That's my father, I would know that cough anywhere. He died of emphysema.'

'Are you sure?' I asked.

'Definitely, it was my father.'

We listened to the rest of the tape but there was nothing but the waves of the energies – which sounded like the sea crashing against rocks.

We tried to listen to the cough again but it had vanished.

I could not understand why a spirit entity should go to so much trouble to make a recording only to have it wiped out after one hearing. However, although this was a complete mystery, it did not take away the magic.

Voices were not the only things that were recorded. At various times I heard music, tapping, singing – albeit it very faint – a humming sound, a dog barking, a bell ringing. I was never sure what I was going to hear next. I became a tape recorder addict.

Throughout the whole of these years, the phenomena I had experienced from the beginning were still there and, I must admit, there were times when I thought it was all too much. I could not understand why the spirits were still so active, after all, I had given in long ago. I simply did not have the time to give each individual happening my utmost attention. For instance, I would have liked to be able to pay more attention to the funnel of light in my hall that appeared almost every day. Why was it there? Who were the entities that sometimes appeared inside it? What did they want? I needed an answer to all of these questions. And especially to the most important question of all. Where was it all leading?

Like the ever-changing faces on the walls I too was changing dramatically. There was a light in my eyes that had not been there before and, for the first time in my life, I was at ease with myself. Although I had never been obsessed by the fear of death, there had obviously been times when I had thought about it, especially when I had been critically ill. Now I no longer looked on death as an end, but simply as a re-birth, mirroring our physical birth. There are people waiting to hug and love you when you finally emerge from the dark birth canal into the light and it is the same when one spins into the dark tunnel and goes toward the light. There we are met by our friends, relatives and our spiritual guides.

Although I had taught hand analysis, and vitamin and mineral therapy, I had never thought that I would be talking about spiritual matters but had, quite unconciously, assumed that role. I was asked so many questions that it became unavoidable.

I must confess that there were times when I had to laugh at my ever-changing role in life, and I asked myself, over and over again where it was all leading?

I had to leave all my questions in abeyance as the relentless phenomena continued. Whilst healing, my attention was frequently drawn to the limbs of my patients, which were being manipulated by unseen hands. Very often the patient was asleep, but there were times when they themselves drew my attention to this. It was fascinating to watch, and the recipient could actually feel the hands that were controlling the proceedings. There were times when I could see the hands, but I was so drawn to the physical manipulations that my spiritual vision was blocked. It became a regular occurrence for a friend or relative of the patient to feel spirit hands on parts of their own body whilst they sat waiting. It was wonderful in so many ways, for it brought a tremendous amount of laughter to my healing room. Very often, someone would say, 'I can't believe this, someone has their hands on my legs.' When this happened I would receive a diagnosis. At other times people would arrive for healing in groups and were amazed as they watched each other being manipulated simultaneously. They could all feel the hands at work and, at one time, seven people were receiving this treatment. So obviously there were seven spirits working together. It never ceased to amaze me.

Naturally, stories of this phenomenon spread, so much so that my answering machine simply could not take the strain. In those days they were not as efficient as they are now. Also, the strain on my own energy resources began to take its toll, and the only way I could refresh myself was to spend Sunday morning in bed. What a joy! But something always seemed to interrupt my reverie. One Sunday I heard water trickling down the wall behind my bed. 'Oh no!' I thought. 'A tile must have come off the roof.' Then, as I listened more intently, the trickle turned into the sound of rushing water, I sat up in bed and looked at the wall behind my bed. It was completely dry. I made my way up intto Janet's bedroom, which was above mine, but there was no water, no leaks of any kind. Still in my dressing gown, I went into the attic. Turning on the light I was able to see that my fears were completely unfounded. I stopped at intervals, as I made my way downstairs, to see if I could still hear the water, but there was nothing. I went back to my bedroom and sat on the bed. The noise had stopped, so I jumped back into bed – but after a few minutes the trickling noise started again and became a gushing sound as though a tap had been turned full on. What on earth did it mean? I was completely nonplussed. I often had some idea of why I was receiving a certain kind of phenomenon, but not this time. Rather irreverently, I played around with the idea that as I was a Piscean, someone was providing water for the two fishes in my star sign. If it were not for my sense of humour, I really do not think I could have put up with the continual interference in my life.

Then I thought of my father, who had drowned when I was only sixteen. Why did his memory suddenly seem so vivid? He had been dead for over thirty years, and I had not thought about him for a long time. Perhaps that was it! He did not want me to forget him, and he was manifesting the sound of water, as it was so significant at the time of his death. I remember, about six months after his death, waking up and finding him standing by my bed. I screamed and my mother came in and comforted me, assuring me that it was only a bad dream, but I knew otherwise. He was as solid as he had been when he was alive. Thinking about this experience now, I realized that he was just trying to show us that he had survived.

Although his mother was a brilliant medium the subject was never brought up in our home as my mother was, quite frankly, terrified of the idea.

I will never really know whether my assumptions about the sounds of water were correct, but it comforts me to think that it was my father, and from that time I promised myself that I would never forget him. As I write these words I can feel his presence.

This was the first of many such events that I was to experience on my so called day of rest. *Always on a Sunday* could have been my theme song!

I was horrified to find one morning, on waking, that I could not move my body, and that my arms and legs were paralysed. My first thought was 'don't panic', but I did. Immediately, I felt the familiar tingle of energy rushing through my body and then my limbs were alive with 'pins and needles'. I tried to get out of bed but standing on my feet was agony, so I waited until all the sensations had gone. Eventually my body returned to normal and I was able to walk around freely, although I still felt dizzy and had an 'out of the body' feeling.

I decided to tackle the housework – for me a boring, soul-destroying task, but one that ensured that I would stay earthbound. It worked! Nevertheless, the memory of my temporary paralysis still invaded my thoughts at times. 'Would it happen again?' I asked myself. Why had it happened? These thoughts and many more were dancing around in my head. I wondered whether the psychic part of my life was damaging my physical body. For the first time ever I was afraid to go to bed that night for fear of what might happen when I woke in the morning. My fears, however, were unfounded.

Two weeks later, whilst I was meditating, my spiritual teacher spoke to me and explained what had happened.

'When you are in a deep sleep, your mind leaves your body, and, although it is still attached to the physical by an energy umbilical cord, it is free to travel. If the journey has been long, you may awake before the mind has fully returned to the body. That is what happened to you.'

'Supposing the umbilical cord breaks?' I asked.

'It can only be severed by the total breakdown of the physical body,' he replied.

I was delighted by this short explanation, and it laid to rest the fear that I still felt before going to bed.

At last, everything was falling into place, and it had begun to make such good sense. The realization dawned on me that it was, in fact, a psychic science, bordering on physics. It was an exciting idea.

But there was something else that was bothering me. I was working so hard that I seemed to be more out of this world than in it. I decided to have a gathering of the clans, so to speak, friends with like minds who would understand my need to 'let go' and earth myself for a few hours. After I had made a few phone calls, the date was set for the following weekend.

Meanwhile, I had been practising remote viewing. I had an urge, one day, to paint the inside of a circular tin tray with black paint and prop it up on a small table where, in my quieter moments, I would just sit and stare at it. Nothing much happened for about two months, and then one day I saw the tray fill with a white, swirling energy. Within minutes, this had turned into a vortex which fascinated me so much that I lost all sense of time and place. Eventually the vortex opened up, and before me was a tunnel with a light at the end. It was as though I was looking through binoculars. And then, to my amazement, I could see one of the friends I had invited to my party. He was wearing an old dressing gown and worn slippers, and looked thoroughly down at heel. He walked through a door with a cup of tea in his hand. Then the energy evaporated and I was left looking at my black tin tray. I could not believe what I had seen. I knew this man extremely well, and he was one of the best dressed men in my circle. It was inconceivable that he would walk around indoors looking like a tramp. I decided, for a bit of fun, to bide my time and challenge him with the picture I had received.

The day of the party arrived, and everyone was having fun. Later, when we were sitting around talking about our lives, I turned to the man and described what I had seen. Everyone laughed, and said that I needed more practice, as it could not have possibly been him.

'You must be joking,' one friend said. 'He's the best dressed man I know.' Turning to his wife, she said, jokingly, 'It's your duty to defend him.'

His wife was laughing uncontrollably. 'I told him he'd be found out one day, but he was so sure no one would ever see him in his old togs.'

Everyone was looking at him in amazement, 'Do you really look like that indoors?' they asked.

His wife answered for him, 'Yes, he does,' she said. 'The dressing gown belonged to his father and he won't throw it away, and he refuses to throw those old slippers away too, because he insists that all his cares and woes disappear when he wears them.' She threw up her hands in mock dismay, and said, 'Now that Betty has discovered your secret you'll have to do something about it.' Her husband smiled. 'No I won't,' he said. 'I have less to worry about now that they all know.'

He didn't mind at all that we spent the rest of the evening pulling his leg, we had all been friends for too long for him to be upset, but he made us take a vow of silence, so that his secret would not reach his business acquaintances.

'Let's face it,' I said, 'the only place you can relax these days is at home.' I also confessed to looking like a tramp when I was alone. This made him feel better.

'One last thing,' I asked. 'Why did I see you walking around with a cup of tea in your hand?'

'Because,' he explained, pointing to his wife, 'she had gone to bed early, with a headache, and I was fetching and carrying for her all evening. That included taking her endless cups of tea.'

I was thrilled that my first remote pictures had been correct, but could not understand why I had linked into that particular friend – unless it was because his wife was unwell and my healing energies had automatically linked into their household. It was also further proof of the mind's ability to travel through space. It was becoming blatantly obvious to me that if we do not free our minds, we cannot link in with the Universal Mind and the knowledge that is there for the taking. We owe it to ourselves to seek knowledge and, with that knowledge, to try to make this world a better place to live in. It was with this in mind that I decided to push my experience one step further by trying astral travel.

Once or twice, over the years, I had felt my mind leaving my body but I was disciplined enough to be able to pull back. I had a fear of 'letting go', but the idea of an energy umbilical cord gave me the courage to explore further. In the next chapter you can read about my explorations into the unknown.

CHAPTER EIGHT

FEELING EXHAUSTED AT THE END of a twelve hour working day, I decided to replenish my energies by lying down on my medical couch and to ask for healing. In the next instant I felt as though I was being lifted off the couch, and a white mist was swirling toward me. At least, that is how it appeared at first. But it was not long before I realized that it was actually the reverse. I was spinning towards the mist, and had the impression that I was being pulled through a vortex. Then I found myself floating high above the earth, drifting over the most magnificent scenery of green fields, valleys, mountains, rivers and lakes. The sun was shining in a blue sky and fluffy clouds scurried below. I cannot remember having any conscious thoughts at all; I only knew that I was in a wonderful world of movement and total serenity and wanted to stay. Alas, this was not to be. The sun disappeared, and the blue sky was obliterated by black clouds, and I snapped back into my body. Snapped! That was the word; it describes exactly the feeling when my mind returned to my body.

I opened my eyes and looked around the room. I asked myself if I could have been dreaming. Then thought for a moment and decided that it had *not* been a dream. I had been on my first astral flight, and it had been fantastic. I closed my eyes again and tried to recreate the experience, but nothing happened. I wanted to defy gravity and fly like a bird, but I felt like lead as my mind refused to leave for a second time. Desperately disappointed, I swung myself off the couch – and as my feet touched the floor I realized that I had indeed been rejuvenated. I felt marvellous for the next few days, my mind was fully occupied with the thought of astral travel. I had often felt, whilst meditating, that a little push would send me on my way, but it had actually taken me completely by surprise. It had not been a journey where one gradually picked up speed and then whoosh! I had just had the whoosh! Without any warning at all. But how was I to do it by myself?

For about a month I tried many different methods of meditating, but although I sometimes had a feeling of 'lift off' nothing happened. Eventually I became bored by the whole procedure, especially as so many other exciting things were happening all around me. Then, out of the blue, it happened again – but this time I was transported to a different country.

I had been giving healing to a child who lived in Marbella, Spain, and on this particular morning had received a letter from her mother telling me that the doctors had not given the little girl very long to live. I was looking at the address and room number of the hospital whilst giving the child absent healing, when I had the same 'lift off' feeling as before. This time, however, I found myself standing in a hospital room looking down on the child. It felt perfectly natural that I should be there. I noticed a crucifix and rosary on the table by the side of the bed. The little girl was asleep and looked very pale. I have no recollection of how long I stood there, but I can remember feeling exhilarated by the thought that she was going to recover. Then, once again, I snapped back into my body. I wrote to the mother telling her that I had been with her daughter in spirit, and asked whether she would confirm that there had been a crucifix and rosary on the bedside table. A month later I received a reply to my letter and the mother confirmed my observation. She also told me that her daughter had made a miraculous recovery. As I read the letter the memory of the visit became crystal clear, and I remember thinking as I had stood in the hospital room that it was as though all the thoughts and prayers of the world were merging, bringing healing to the sick child. From that day, I have never believed that praying was a waste of time. The thought is the deed.

I was disturbed by the fact that I was still not in control of these astral travels. Was someone supervising the journeys? I was completely in the dark; I had hoped that I would be given spiritual guidance, there was only silence. It was at times like these that I became totally frustrated. I did not know whether to pursue a course of constructive meditations, to elicit astral journeys, or to do nothing. There was no doubt that I was hooked on the idea. It was no wonder, I thought, that spirit entities were so happy when they gave survival evidence. They had the opportunity to fly all the time!

Absent healing was responsible for the many times I found myself standing at the foot of a bed looking down on a sick person. But after six months I was still waiting to experience, once again, that incredible sensation of flying. I needed to see the mountains and valleys again, and feel the peace and serenity that cloaked me during that flight. I was certain of one thing, however, and that was the need for discipline if I was ever to be successful with astral travel. Self-control is required in meditation but I knew instinctively that it had to go beyond that. I was convinced that once having triggered my first astral flight I would always have that ability. But how to do it?

I decided to spend half an hour each day practising different forms of meditation. Once or twice, during the first month, I nearly succeeded) and tantalizing glimpses of scenery appeared. But they were short-lived. However, it did confirm my belief that the only obstacle was my inability to let go, to allow my mind to be free.

This knowledge led me to the next phase. During my healing sessions I regularly went into trance, and it was during these times, when my mind energy was partially out of my body, that spirit doctors linked 'mind to mind' and worked through me. It occurred to me that if I allowed myself to imitate a trance-like state whilst I was alone, then perhaps my mind energy would be able to fly.

My first attempts were a total failure. Then, quite by chance, I found myself thinking of a young man who was seriously ill in Spain. Without any preparation, I found myself high in the sky looking down on the landscape below. I did not, at that moment, think about how I had achieved it, because when one is completely out of the body it seems to be so normal. Finally, I found myself in a room full of people for what seemed like only a second, and then I was back home, opening my eyes. The return felt very gentle and I did not have the same 'snapped back' feeling as before. I thought about the people I had seen. Were they the young man's family? Or had I simply dropped in on strangers? I decided to write to my patient, explaining what had happened, and ask him whether he had any idea who these people were. A week later, he wrote to tell me that it had been his birthday on that day, and his family had arranged a party for him. I am pleased to say that, after a long, drawn out illness, he fully recovered.

What had I done to achieve my aim? Surely astral travel could not be that easy – and if it was, how was I going to control it? Then, suddenly, I knew! *Control.* My flights were being controlled by someone other than myself, and if I trusted my guardian and did not try to take charge of the situation myself, all would be well.

It became obvious to me, as in everything else connected to my mediumship, that this new phenomenon was not for my own pleasure, but to enable me to visit sick people. And what I had to do was to keep out of the way and allow my guide to do his work. How did I know it was a male? Because he accompanied me on one particular flight.

Astral flights of this nature only occur when someone is suffering a deep trauma of some kind. But I found as time went on, that I was able to take similar flights through visualization.

My own experiences led me to believe that anyone who is not spiritually guided in other aspects of their life should not attempt astral travel. The following story illustrates this.

I was invited to give healing at a centre in Madrid, and understood that other healers would also be present. As I had lived in Spain for some years and could speak the language, I agreed. On arrival, I hired a cab to take me to the centre. As we neared our destination I saw a long queue of people lining the pavement, and my first thought was that there must be a popular film being shown in the local cinema. Imagine my surprise when I learned that they were all waiting to see me, as the other healers had, for various reasons, failed to turn up. In fact, I soon learned that they had cancelled their trip altogether. The situation seemed hopeless as there was only one Spanish lady at the centre, and she could not speak a word of English. I realized that it would take me all day and night to be able to help these people, but there was nothing I could do but get on with it. To save time, I told them that I would be healing them in groups of four or five at a time.

But as the day went by I became increasingly concerned. Not by the ordinary complaints that one sees all the time, but by the fact that nice ordinary people had been hoodwinked into paying astronomical sums of money to be taught how to travel on the astral plane. They had also had a guarantee that they could achieve this in the first lesson, and as a result, there had been many casualties, and people had been left with severe afflictions because of the forced nature of the astral travel sessions. They had been given no spiritual guidance, and the course had been based on nothing but sensationalism.

Because of my ability to see 'mind energy', I was able to diagnose each person individually, and treat them accordingly. When they left I gave them some simple exercises to keep themselves earthed. If I had been unable to see the mind energy and manipulate it into the normal shape, I dread to think what might have happened to them.

One particularly distressing case was that of a young girl who, having forced the mind energy halfway out of her body, could not bring it back. She was sobbing all the time, her balance disturbed, she swayed when she tried to walk, and she was convinced that she was going mad. I placed my hands upon her head for about ten minutes, and then gradually eased the mind energy into position. Within twenty minutes she was back to normal. I wanted her never to experiment in these matters again, and sent her away with a couple of earthing exercises.

There are many people who have experienced spontaneous astral travel only once in their lives and have been happy to leave it at that. They are the sensible ones. There are others, like myself, who want to relive the sensations of flight, and to see, once again, the spectacular scenery. If you belong in the latter group, don't even think about it. It can be dangerous. I was lucky because as a medium, I was protected from my own stupidities. But I also learned from them. I hope those readers who are interested in astral flight will take heed of this cautionary tale.

Meditation is undoubtedly the safest way of achieving mind expansion. In the meditational exercises that I have devised over the years, the meditator is always in control, and it is a disciplined process that can only bring health and happiness. Without the pressure on the brain and body, the energy system is able to release the blockages and bring new life to all the vital organs. It is the best anti-stress treatment I know.

Throughout my life I have used meditation as a way of coping with pressure. In retrospect, I realize that I was guided to the subjects I chose to study, and that the regular expansion of my mind enabled me to absorb the information and guidance.

That is probably why I have received such incredible phenomena. The mind, once free, can help us to free ourselves from the bonds of our physical bodies.

Unlike astral travel, one can meditate every day, and – with visualization – this enables us to visit the most wonderful places. And as you have your finger on the control button you can return whenever you wish. The more you meditate, the clearer the pictures will become and the more you will be able to 'feel' the atmosphere. Whatever methods you use to reach your destination, use the same method to return.

In my meditation and anti-stress workbook, *Betty Shine's Mind Workbook*, there is an extensive list of exercises to suit whatever mood you may be in at the time. They are especially helpful in enabling each individual to become independent of outside help as the self-help factor gradually takes over. The question most people ask me in their letters is, 'What happens if we go to sleep whilst listening to your tapes?' There is no need to worry about this, for once you are asleep you will absorb the healing and information automatically, and your mind will act accordingly.

It seems to me that human beings are becoming control freaks, especially since the invention of the computer. Like every new discovery, this has brought with it both good and bad. The biggest problem, eventually, is the inability to let go.

Meditation is the easiest way I know of letting go, even when one is going through a bad patch. But it does help to know that because the mind depresses the brain and compresses the body when in a negative state, this in turn will lead to physical disorders. This knowledge should encourage you to reverse the process by practising positivity and relaxation. Remember, whatever your thoughts are, they will directly affect your health. The following story serves to illustrate this.

A man, in his forties came to me for healing and, as soon as I looked at his energies, I could see that he was physically crippled and mentally troubled. I encouraged him to speak to me whilst I gave him healing. At first he was reluctant to do so, but as he relaxed, he told me that his wife had left him and wanted a divorce.

'The problem is, I still love her,' he said.

'What do you think caused her to leave?' I asked.

'Oh, my work, definitely,' he replied. 'You see, I'm a salesman and I'm never at home.'

'Can't you change your job?' I asked, 'After all your marriage should come first.'

He grimaced. 'I've tried, but I can't do anything else.'

He was looking so dejected that I changed the subject and explained why he was in such bad physical shape. I told him that no matter what situation he found himself in, he could not afford to be negative.

'Sometimes,' I said, 'we have to remove the obstacles so that we can get on with our lives and remain healthy. If you find that you cannot remove them, then you must find a positive angle to the problem.'

'What do you mean?' he asked.

'First of all,' I said, 'I would like to ask you if you are being really truthful with yourself when you tell me that your job is the reason for the separation. It could be that you are blaming it on your occupation to avoid the real issue.'

He looked slightly annoyed by this suggestion. 'I don't know what you're getting at,' he said.

I smiled, trying to lighten the tension. 'Well, for instance, did you let your wife know how much you missed her whilst you were away from home?'

'She knows I miss her,' he replied.

I pressed on. 'Yes, but do you *tell* her? Make a fuss of her? It's the little things that make such a difference to a woman's life.'

'No! When I get home I'm too bloody tired to think of anything but my bed,' he replied.

Trying to get my point across to him, I said, 'But did you pay her a lot of attention once you'd rested?'

He frowned. 'Not really! I didn't think I had to. We've been married for ten years.'

'Look,' I explained. 'It's my job to know these things. During the healing, I picked up that it was an emotional issue between yourself and your wife, and not the job. That is why I've been encouraging you to recognize this factor yourself, and not take the easy path by blaming your job. If you could get rid of the apathy that has apparently been creeping up on you for some time, I think it would go a long way to solving your problem.'

He thought for a moment, then said, 'Okay! It isn't going to be easy, but I'll try.'

I laughed. 'Who promised us that life would be easy?'

He came to see me for the next five weeks, and changed considerably in that time, even though his wife resolutely refused to consider a reconciliation. She had obviously had enough!

Two years later he married for the second time, and brought his new wife to see me. He was a completely different man, both mentally and physically. As he was leaving, he turned to me and said, 'You were right, you know, and I'll make sure I don't make the same mistakes again.'

I met them at a restaurant four years later, and they still looked extremely happy.

I am continually amazed by the fact that married couples find it so very difficult to assure each other of their love. One of the major causes is embarrassment, and this is most apparent in men, who simply do not seem to think that their partner needs reassurance on a regular basis. Whenever this problem arises, the standard answer from most men is, 'Why does she need reassurance? I married her, didn't I?' Although this is often said half-jokingly, there is a strong feeling on the part of the male that marriage says it all. On behalf of all the frustrated women I have met, I have to say that it doesn't. There are so many ways to show someone that you love them, and showing that love becomes easier with practice. Have a go!

CHAPTER NINE

T HE LAST FIVE YEARS HAD BEEN INCREDIBLE. Although I had known instinctively that something sensational was going to happen sometime in my life, nothing on earth would have convinced me that it was going to be of a paranormal nature. And yet, in retrospect, it is difficult to understand why this had never occurred to me, especially as I had been seeing spirits since the age of two. It was possibly because I had become engrossed in an operatic career, as well as looking after a young family, and so the psychic part of me had to take a back seat.

When I was finally made aware of my gift, and accepted it, the spirit world probably celebrated and said, 'At last! She has woken up.' The first medium I visited had said, 'There are many people who wish to work through you, and you have refused to accept your destiny.' To be honest, I did not understand this statement at the time. I have always embraced knowledge with open arms, so perhaps there had been something wrong with their communcations system!

The spirits could have been forgiven for thinking that I was stubborn; after I had found out about my psychic abilities I was, most definitely, a reluctant medium. Although I was coming to terms with the fact that psychic talents cannot and should not be separated, there was that old enemy – time. I felt that healing should be given priority over sittings, and I still feel that way. I also knew that spirit communicators would be more than happy to convey their messages whilst I was healing. Some people, unfortunately, insisted that they did not require healing and were upset when I said that I was too busy to give them separate sittings. Although I regularly asked for guidance on this matter, the problem remained with me for some time until one day, a lady asked if she could accompany her friend who was to receive healing. I agreed. When they arrived I took them into the healing room and suggested that the friend relaxed in an armchair in the corner of the room. I had been healing for about twenty minutes when I heard someone whispering. I looked up and there, standing behind the armchair, were two spirit entities. They told me their names were Ethel and Nan and that they were aunts of the friend sitting in the chair. I was able to describe their dress in detail, and the fact that one of them was wearing an emerald choker. When I mentioned the necklace the friend froze in her seat. She sat looking at me as though she had seen a ghost.

Then Ethel said, pointing to the choker, 'This was left to you.' Family history and names were mentioned to verify that they were, indeed, who they claimed to be. It was only when Ethel and Nan had gone that I realized that the mediumship and healing could be given simultaneously.

The recipient of the survival messages was still looking slightly dazed.

'My sister and I were brought up by the aunts,' she explained. 'Ethel had told me many times during my childhood that I would inherit the choker, and Nan had promised my sister that she would have her diamond ring.' She smiled, as the memories came flooding back. 'We loved them so much and really did not care whether they left us anything or not. As far as we were concerned they were never going to die. But, obviously, they did.' The friend looked at me, and went on tearfully, 'Ethel went first and Nan died three months later. I don't think they could bear to be without each other.'

'What happened to the jewellery?' I asked.

'Unfortunately they never left a will, and although we told the rest of the family about their bequest, it was ignored, and an elder brother claimed everything. That's why I can understand her frustration now. He couldn't have cared less about them whilst they were alive.'

'Did they leave you their home?' I asked.

'No,' she replied, 'the house was rented. But we were able to afford the rent between us, and the landlord allowed us to stay on.'

I was puzzled. 'Why didn't Nan speak out about the ring?'

'My sister was fortunate enough to have received backing from a relative on that issue, and was given the ring. But the choker was sold for a very considerable sum of money.'

We talked for a while and, when they were ready to leave, she said, 'You've killed two birds with one stone today. I was going to ask you for a sitting.'

This gave me an idea. Friends often wished to visit me together, and I was frequently asked to give healing to one and a sitting to the other. I decided, in future, to ask whether they would like to share the hour. I explained that if there were to be any survival messages, they would come through during the healing. If there were no messages, then time would have not been wasted for either of us. And it worked! At least sixty per cent of friends were willing to share their experiences, and I had time to give private sittings to the rest. Perfect!

During one of these shared meetings I began to explain my theories on mind energy. During a visit from a lady called Joan, I demonstrated how the hand could be used as a magnet by placing it on her head and then gently pulling it away.

'There you are,' I said. 'You should feel lighter now the compression has gone.

'Betty!' she gasped.

'Yes, what is it?' I asked.

'It is my father. There, in the corner of the room,' she replied.

Following her gaze, I saw a man dressed in old clothes holding a straw hat. He was smiling.

'Can you see him?' Joan asked.

'Yes.'

'Oh!' she said. 'I can't see him any more, he's gone.'

Joan looked dumbstruck. 'That was definitely my father,' she told me. 'He was a teacher, and his favourite outfit was his gardening clothes and straw hat.' She looked at me earnestly and asked, 'Did he say anything?'

'No, I'm afraid he didn't,' I said.

'I have never seen a spirit before. Why was I able to see one today?' she wondered.

'It was because I had expanded your mind energy. You only see spirits with your mind, because it's made up of the same components as they are.'

Her friend, who had been receiving healing, was sitting on the couch looking completely bewildered. 'Do you mean to say that if you did the same thing to me I would be able to see spirit people?'

'I doubt it,' I replied. 'These things happen spontaneously, and rarely happen twice unless one is a medium. You see mediums have naturally expansive mind energies. When they close their eyes and relax, it expands further, enabling them not only to see but hear.'

'Why didn't my father speak to me?' Joan asked.

'He was probably as surprised as you were that you were able to see him.' I told her that friends and relatives are often around, but the majority of people cannot see them.

Helen, my patient, said, 'I think you're right. I've been told by many people that they have felt their parents near them after they have died.' She sighed. 'I would love to be able to see my mother again.'

'Well, maybe you will, especially if you meditate regularly.'

I had been thrilled by this experience, not only for Joan, but for myself as well. It was being proved to me time and again that my theories were correct.

I had been told on several occasions that patients had seen someone standing by them while they were receiving healing. Now and then they would recognize a relative, and the joy on their face was a sight to behold. The complete simplicity and naturalness of the moment also surprised them.

It had become common knowledge amongst my patients that this phenomenon was likely to happen. Unfortunately, it was not as frequent as they would have liked, causing some disappointment.

It was, however, happening more frequently to those who had asked for absent healing. I received letters and phone calls every week telling me stories of loved ones who had appeared to them during the hours of healing – some for a split second, while others stayed for a few minutes. Even pets they had lost could be seen. The explanation is simple: when receiving healing the energies are raised, in some more than others, and those who could see spirits were viewing them with an expanded 'mind energy'. It is especially successful if you are linking in with a powerful healer, for it is that boost of energy that frees the mind.

One day, I received a letter from South Africa. It was from a lady called Bella, who was in her eighties. We had been corresponding for over a year, and she had been delighted with the healing she had received. In this particular letter she told me that her late mother, father, and two sisters had appeared to her whilst she was linking in with me. At first she had closed her eyes, but then sensed that she should open them. When she did, her family were standing there before her. She had thought at first that she was dreaming – or that she had died.

'Betty,' she wrote, 'I still can't believe it happened. I was looking straight at them'. Bella died three years later, and I am sure all her family were waiting to meet her.

As far as my own life was concerned, spirits were still appearing every day, in some form or another. Sometimes there would be a wisp of energy that resembled a human form, another time the entity would be physical, and distinguished from a living person only by trails of energy that swirled around the floor. Another type would be a beautiful human, but totally transparent. The hands that appeared over my patients when I was giving healing nearly always looked solid, making it easy for the patients to feel the pressure when they were touched.

I was woken, one night, by a bright light shining in my eyes. I thought at first that it was an intruder, but soon realized that the light was not man-made. Silver beams were moving around the room, and the walls appeared to be made of glass. Then I heard a voice say, 'The secret of everlasting life – is love.' The silver beams vanished and my bedroom returned to normal. 'What an enigmatic thing to say,' I thought. Love had always been the most important factor in my life, and I had always known that the immune system is weakened when one is unloved. But there were all kinds of love. Love, the secret of everlasting life: what sort of love *is* it? I had to wait a little longer before I received the answer.

There was one sort of love that I was able to witness on a daily basis, and which thrilled an enormous amount of people. Friends and relatives accompanying a patient would often feel spirit hands on them whilst I was healing. They would say, 'Betty, someone's holding my ankles.' Or, 'I can feel someone's hands on my head.' This phenomenon suddenly escalated to such a degree that I was no longer surprised by it. And the fact that several spirit healers worked on different people in the room at the same time convinced me that this was a demonstration of a totally unselfish love. It was very moving, and was a love that changed many lives.

I have met many men who were quite cynical about the benefits of healing, and who had only accompanied their wives under duress. The subject of mediums was definitely taboo; in fact, the wife usually asked me in advance not to mention it. I have to admit that I found it quite funny when the husbands received healing from unseen hands, and enjoyed seeing their expressions as they sat rigid, eyes popping, and rendered totally speechless. I usually gave them a diagnosis whilst they were recovering from the shock. This had a very strange effect on some of them. Still struggling to hold onto their scepticism, they accused their wives of disclosing their problem to me beforehand. On the whole, these sessions were fun, and the men enjoyed the leg-pulling as much as I did. There were many converts. As one gentleman said, 'I will never doubt that there is an afterlife again.'

I always made it quite clear that I was not seeking converts; I did not see that as my role at all. I was usually quite at ease with the sceptics, as I was with those who had faith. I believe that those people who have open minds have a very precious gift; they can embrace all knowledge and have a lifetime to arrive at their conclusion. I find people with closed minds very boring. They seem to arrive at a conclusion and stick to it doggedly for the rest of their lives. Moreover, they can never acknowledge that they might be wrong.

One such person was a man who was so agnostic that I found his presence quite disturbing. About fifteen minutes into the healing, he shouted, 'Bloody hell, I can feel hands around my ankle!' He was terrified.

'It is your left ankle,' I told him calmly. 'You have damaged your achilles heel.'

He was extremely angry. 'How the hell do you know that.' Pointing to his wife, who was by now looking very uncomfortable, he said accusingly, 'I suppose you told her.'

I found his words and actions so unbelievable that I had to cover my face with my hands to hide my laughter. I decided to leave the room for a few minutes to recover. When I returned he had calmed down and, looking a bit sheepish, asked me for an explanation. I told him that when the energies in the room are raised during the healing, the energy counterpart of the body loosens, enabling the recipient of the healing to feel the hands of the spirit entities. I also explained that they never wasted their time healing those who were completely well.

Before he left he was gracious enough to apologize for his behaviour, but admitted that he had received quite a shock. I told him I could understand his reaction.

'Well, someone cared enough to shake you out of your complacency,' I said with a smile.

He grimaced. 'They did that, all right.'

His wife later told me that his scepticism had made her very unhappy for many years, as she had always believed in the afterlife and healing, and that she had prayed that one day he would share her beliefs. Her prayers had finally been answered.

'He is a changed man,' she told me. 'He's read all my books on the subject, and has even bought some himself.'

I am always surprised when I read or listen to supposedly learned people talking absolute rubbish about the paranormal, and remember these words, written by a famous philosopher: 'The greatest critics are those that know nothing about the subject.'

I had by this time gained an enormous amount of confidence, and was no longer disconcerted by any adverse comments that might be directed at me. I have also been blessed with a sense of humour; indeed, the gift of laughter has been the greatest asset in my life, and when faces appeared on the wall – by now another common occurrence – I found myself laughing out loud. It just seemed so ridiculous to have my wall used as a giant screen by an unseen projector.

Relaxing one evening after a particularly busy day, I watched in amazement as the profile of a very dear friend built up on the wall. Then a voice said, 'He needs you.' The profile disappeared and re-appeared at five minute intervals. Smiling to myself, I could imagine his incredulity if I was to phone him and say 'Hi! this is Betty. I'm now a medium, and I'm ringing because I've seen your face building up on the wall.' The more I thought about it the more hilarious it became. Then the voice spoke again. 'He has had an accident, and is in need of your healing.' This did disturb me.

I hesitated to call him, as we had not been in contact with each other for about seven years. I had been living in Spain for many years and, when I returned, the mediumship had taken over my life. I decided to take my time thinking about the situation. The spirits, however, did not approve of this decision and the profile of my friend appeared on every wall in my home. It was obvious that they thought immediate action was necessary.

I picked up the phone and called him. The next part of the story is described by my friend himself.

Many years ago, I had the privilege of being Betty's singing teacher. We had not met, or even spoken to each other, for seven years, when, quite out of the blue, she called me. My partner answered the phone, and I heard him say, 'No! This is Stewart.'

Then he said, 'Good heavens! Betty, Betty Shine! I thought you were still living in Spain. How are you?' Betty apparently asked about my health, because I heard Stewart say, 'If you had asked me that question two days ago I could have told you that David was very well, but I'm afraid that the situation has changed since then.'

There was a pause, and then he said, 'How could you know that?' Apparently, she had told him that she was now a healer, and that her spirit guides had told her about my accident. I remember Stewart asking her if we could call her back later that day. It was quite extraordinary. I had fallen the previous day, and had injured my arm and thumb very seriously. After having had them set, I was required to stay overnight in the hospital. The next day Stewart collected me and brought me home. I had only been in the flat for a few minutes when Betty called.

I later spoke to Betty for some time, and at the end of our conversation she told me that she was giving me healing.

I retired to bed that evening in some considerable pain. I was also extremely worried by the fact that the doctors had not held out much hope of my recovering the full use of my arm and thumb. This disability would seriously affect my work.

I was woken up in the middle of the night with the most extraordinary sensation in my arm. Then I endured a series of quite violent manipulations – and had no control over my arm at at this time. I could find no explanation for this phenomenon at all.

The next morning I called Betty and told her what had happened. She simply laughed! and said! 'Oh! That was my spirit doctor. These manipulations are all part and parcel of the healing process.' I was extremely impressed, especially as my arm and thumb quickly returned to normal.

I was particularly thrilled to have been able to help David, as he had been such a source of inspiration to me in the past and it was the nicest way I knew of saying, 'thank you'.

I had from time to time been asked to co-operate with experiments that were being carried out by scientists and doctors. I did this whenever possible, but the experiment and results were always kept secret and this attitude bored me to tears. Also, on several occasions, I felt that my intellect was being abused. How on earth do these people expect to make things happen when they have no idea what they are tampering with?

There were one or two scientists who were open-minded enough to admit that although they did not understand psychic energy, they were convinced that it existed. I tried to explain that we simply do not know enough about these energies to be able to evaluate them correctly, and as they were not interested in having an intelligent rapport with the medium it all seemed such a waste of time and energy. I found the whole process so dreary. I preferred the instantaneous phenomena, which was more exciting, and if I could not prove the existence of another dimension to the whole world, then I certainly would not lose any sleep over it.

Most phenomena are spontaneous for the simple reason that everything has to be just right for it to happen. Mediums usually have a feeling that something is about to happen, but this is only after many years of working in this field. But then, when you think you are beginning to understand, it changes – that is why the mystery remains unsolved for the moment. Every day I was intrigued by new happenings, and so I decided to make use of my clairvoyant sight, and study the energy that was constantly appearing in my home in one form or another.

It is extremely difficult, I know, for those people who do not have clairvoyant sight to understand those that do. Mediums have been the butt of jokes for centuries, and it was the norm not so long ago for the media to stoop to 'medium bashing', as it was called, when there was nothing more newsworthy around. As I had never previously been interested in the paranormal, I was completely unaware of the hostility that surrounded this profession.

An open mind is the secret of life. Allowing your mind the freedom it needs to seek knowledge, and return it to you 'giftwrapped', is the most wonderful experience. The next story is an example of this.

A young lady in her twenties asked me to teach her how to meditate. We met once a week for an hour, meditating and talking. One day she said, 'Whenever I meditate, I visualize mountains and valleys but before I can lose myself in the scenery a totally different picture overshadows it.' Intrigued, I asked her what this was.

'It's a white cottage beside a lake. Then, the sun rises from behind some hills, and the lake begins to dance as the sunlight is reflected upon the waves. It is very beautiful.'

'Anything else?' I enquired.

'No! That's it.'

'Does this scene stay with you during the whole of your meditation period?' I asked.

She thought for a moment. 'Yes, it does,' she said. 'Do you know what it means?'

Pausing to think for a moment, I was given an explanation. 'I think your mind is linking into your future. The fact that the sun is rising over the lake signifies that it hasn't happened yet. In other words, you are giving yourself your own clairvoyance.'

She frowned, then laughed. 'I don't think I want to live with a fisherman,' she said.

I asked her to concentrate on a particular object when she meditated next. She followed my instructions, but the cottage and lake overshadowed everything she tried. Each week there were additions to the picture; first there was a car, then two black dogs, and most significant of all, a ski-lift in the background. Being an adept pupil, she soon learned the art of meditation and continued practising on her own.

Eighteen months later I received a letter from Switzerland. The same young lady was now living in a white cottage on the Italian/Swiss border, on the edge of a lake, with two black dogs, two cars, and from the photograph she had sent me I could see a ski-lift in the background. She had added a PS: 'Why didn't I see both cars? Because the second car was a present from my husband, and it was a secret!'

What was so refreshing about this young lady was the fact that she accepted without reservation everything that she was given. I have no doubt that her own clear vision will enable her to map out a successful future for herself.

It is so easy for others to put you down simply because they cannot share your beliefs and talents. I have seen so many lovely open minded people lose out because they hadn't the courage to combat the cynicism of partners, relatives and close friends.

I was extremely lucky. My family backed me all the way. Although they could not see the spirits themselves, they knew I was of sound mind, and they were often well aware that peculiar things were happening all around them. Doors inexplicably opened then shut of their own accord, and muted voices were heard by everyone, even visitors.

There was always a tremendous amount of phenomena – for all to see – at Christmas, a time which is very special to me. When I lived in Sutton I always had a huge Christmas tree in the hall, decorated with the usual trinkets and flashing lights. Behind the tree a tape recorder played carols. One of my male patients was admiring the scene when he suddenly started to crawl around the tree on all fours.

'Is this some kind of ritual?' I laughingly enquired.

He looked up. 'Are these lights powered by batteries?' he asked .

'No, they're plugged into the socket behind you.'

'Betty, the plug is under the tree. The lights are working without any source of electricity.'

I thought he was pulling my leg, but when I joined him at the back of the tree I could see the plug lying amongst the presents.

'Where the hell is the power coming from?' he asked.

I had no idea.

It was a complete mystery. The lights flashed all day of their own accord and went out at night. The next day, unfortunately, we had to resort to the use of electricity again.

This was the beginning of what I was to call the 'electric phenomena.' I would go into my bedroom and find that the bedside lamps had been switched on. If I had left them on, they would be switched off. Walking into the lounge I would find the television on, with no apparent source of supply, as the plug had been removed from the socket. When I was healing, the light would mysteriously dim until sometimes we were sitting in total darkness. But when I had finished the light would return to normal again. The answerphone would suddenly have a bout of whirring, with occasional bits of conversation drifting in and out of the noise. It suffered a breakdown, as did five other subsequent answering machines. Whilst looking at television one evening, the screen suddenly went blank, and I found myself looking at a man with strange penetrating eyes and peculiar garb. He had a hypnotic effect on me. A few minutes later the programme reappeared. I wondered later whether I had been dreaming, although I knew full well that I had not. After a while that is how these phenomena come to affect you. Living between two worlds all the time is not easy, and not always welcomed. On rare occasions it can be positively disrupting.

One such occasion was when I was entertaining a friend for the evening. I closed the door of the lounge, and we sat down to enjoy our drinks. Within minutes we both heard a creaking sound coming from the other side of the door, and when we looked over, we saw the handle being turned. We knew that there was no one else in the house at the time, and so immediately thought there might be an intruder. My friend picked up a heavy ornament for protection as the door slowly opened, but when we investigated there was no one there. We closed the door, and the same thing happened again. By this time we were both annoyed, and looked in every nook and cranny in the house to make absolutely sure there was no other human being around playing tricks. But there was no one. In all, it happened four times that evening, but I was to be plagued by this particular phenomenon for some time. I wondered why if spirits could walk through doors, this one was turning handles to open the door.

Typical of the trend throughout my mediumship, this experience was the catalyst for a whole range of such happenings. Lying in bed one night I heard two ladies whispering together as the door slowly opened. The energy they brought with them caused my bed to start moving. Although I could not see the spirits, I 'knew' who they were. The previous occupants of my house had been three elderly ladies. In their youth, two had been actresses and a third a dancer. It was only after the death of her two companions that the third had sold up.

I had found masses of newspaper cuttings about all three in the attic and, on reading them, had found that they had been very talented. Artists are often very psychic, and I believe that these two ladies were simply visiting their beloved home, hoping to meet with their friend again.

At first I had found these night-time visits disturbing, and had asked for them to be curtailed. So I was surprised to find later, that they no longer bothered me, mainly because the love these entities brought with them was so tangible that I could almost touch it.

Love! There it was again. That word had become part of my everyday teaching – mainly because I was meeting so many people who felt unloved.

One such person was a middle-aged man who has asked me for healing and counselling. He complained that his family treated him badly, and that his children positively disliked him. I could understand this, as I could 'feel' the aggression which was simmering below the surface. We talked for some time and then he said, 'They should respect me. After all I am the bread-winner.' I suggested that if the breadwinner was unloved then the family could actually be choking on the bread.

He looked at me and said, 'Do you really think I am that bad?'

'I think you might be,' I replied.

'Why?' he asked.

'Because I can feel the aggression within you.'

'You know,' he said, 'not so many years ago, we were a big happy family. I don't know what went wrong.' I was able to give him an account of the past so that he could identify the problem.

He came for healing every week for two months. Although he had been cured of his arthritis in the first two weeks, I guessed that he just wanted a sympathetic listener. On his last visit, he said, 'I like you, you don't give me any bull.' I laughed.

About eighteen months later, he called at the door and handed me a bunch of roses, saying, 'I've made my peace with the wife and kids, thanks to you,' he smiled. 'It took some doing, I can tell you. I had to eat humble pie for the first time in my life, but it was worth it to have them hug me again.'

To feel unloved is terrible. To know that you are unloved because of your own past actions is worse.

It became obvious to me, through survival evidence, that the majority of people felt that their mother had been the only person in their life to have loved them unconditionally. Tears would flow, when their mothers recalled their childhood and sent them messages of love.

Through these encounters I learned of the deep unhappiness caused by uncaring people, from all walks of life. It is true to say that familiarity breeds contempt, and yet it is the people with whom we are familiar, our partners and friends, who keep us going when times are difficult.

Mental cruelty is far more common than physical violence, and it starts from childhood. Almost everyone has practised some form of mental cruelty at some time in their lives, but sensitive human beings will know when they have done wrong. And if they cannot right a wrong, then they can certainly change. But it is the premeditated mental cruelty that goes undetected by those who are not immediately involved. One example of this is when a marriage breaks down and ends in divorce. The perpetrator of the suffering is exposed; the victims have often experienced the most abject misery for many years before they are released.

Emotional difficulties cause much pain. Trying to help those who are going through a divorce is like stepping into a war zone, and yet someone has to be there, standing to one side, otherwise both parties could be dreadfully injured during the battle.

It is never too late to rectify our actions. Many people, before they die, leave letters for those they have treated badly, asking for forgiveness. This eases their passing, and makes it easier for the injured party to forgive.

Whilst giving survival evidence, I have found it is very common for the communicator to ask to be forgiven. Very often, the sitter will say that there is nothing to forgive. When this happens, I am given a graphic account of the deed and the circumstances surrounding it. It may be something quite insignificant, but it became obvious to me over the years that it was extremely important to the person who was now living in a more beautiful and loving environment, and who had obviously been shown the error of their ways.

I had been told many times during survival evidence that when one dies the whole of your life passes before you like tickertape. It is over in what seems to be only seconds, but in that time you are left in no doubt about the havoc you have caused during your lifetime.

It can be argued that it is mainly other people who send us to hell in this life. This is only partly true. We also allow them to do it. Sometimes, as the following story shows, one is unable to do anything about it at the time, for a hundred different reasons. But, as the saying goes, every dog has its day.

Nancy was a conscientious mother of four children, whose ages ranged from four to fourteen. Her husband was an absolute charmer outside of the home, but to his family he was a monster. As well as being a ladies man and a liar, he had, over the years, perfected the art of mental cruelty. I had known them both for many years, and Nancy had been a patient for a year. The healing had eased some of her pain, but she was trapped and they both knew it. First of all, she had no money of her own, and the house was in her husband's name only. On my advice she tried to get help from several organizations but it seemed that no one could ease her suffering. She was not a physically battered wife, and the mental scars did not show.

However, one day a friend offered her a job where she could live in with her children. She turned the offer down admitting to me that she simply did not have the courage to leave. I could understand her reaction, for when one has lived with mental cruelty and rejection for so long, enduring it becomes a habit, and one becomes masochistic. Her life continued in this vein until she became very ill. I had warned her that this would happen. Fortunately her friends removed Nancy and her children from her home and nursed her back to health.

Two years later I met her again. She was brimming over with good health, happy and successful in her own right. Whilst we were talking she admitted that she had made her own life hell by refusing to leave. 'If only I had been more courageous,' she said.

Of course, not everyone has wonderful friends that come like shining knights to the rescue, but we are all capable of using visualization to conjure up pictures of the kind of life we want to lead. We are also capable of planning our escape routes. The only way most of us can cope at times is by escaping into a dream world but, with courage, it could and should materialize in this dimension.

Dream-time is so important to us all. Day-dreaming is the answer for everyone who is overstressed, whether at work or in the home. Unlike meditation, you do not have to prepare yourself, but can simply drift off when you have a moment to spare. You may be thinking about a person, a holiday, an object – a new house, or car for example, the list is endless and the dream is your own.

The only danger comes if you believe that the materialistic dream can become reality without the hard work needed to attain it. Everything gained by deceit of any kind will bring with it a price, and that price will have to be paid when you are at your lowest ebb. That is spiritual law, and is illustrated by the following story.

A young man coveted another man's position within the same firm. He knew how much salary the other man received, and was envious of the rewards that it provided – a nice home, a BMW sports car, and the luxurious holidays with his wife.

The young man began to undermine his superior in small ways, waiting for his chance to pounce when he took his next holiday.

When this happened he conned the bosses into believing that their colleague had been using his power to undermine the firm and pass information onto a similar company. The plan worked, and when his superior returned from holiday he was told to leave.

The young man was eventually given the position he had coveted, and he bought a BMW sports car and tried to emulate the life-style of his ex-colleague. Within a year he had lost the job, the car, and the life-style, when he was found to be totally unsuitable for the position because of his laziness. His lies were unearthed later. He had made the mistake of believing that he could simply reap the rewards of another person's hard work.

Two years later, the business ran into financial difficulties and was saved from bankruptcy by the man he had deceived.

We all have a spiritual log book, and the keeper of that book will only identify themselves when we leave this dimension. It is then, and only then, that the content will be made known to us so that we can redress the balance.

CHAPTER TEN

I HAD BEEN LIVING IN A PSYCHIC CIRCUS for six years now, and it was finally beginning to calm down. The phenomena were more disciplined, which meant that I could plan my time more effectively.

Faces still appeared on the walls, but I was able to recognize them now and act upon them, sometimes preventing a major catastrophe. The following story is about one of these near disasters.

I was standing in the hall of my home when, out of the corner of my eye, I thought I saw something moving. I turned, and saw a swirling mass of energy covering the wall behind me. I stood entranced as the mass was moulded into a face. Even the spectacles were there! I recognized the person immediately, felt the urgency of the message and called the lady in question. There was no answer. I phoned her daughter, who lived nearby, told her what had happened, and asked her to visit her mother to make sure that nothing was amiss. She said that she would leave at once, and promised to call me when she arrived at her mother's home. Two hours passed. I was becoming increasingly disturbed as I linked into the mother, because I was not getting the normal response from her energies that I would have expected. Then her daughter called me. Apparently, she had found her mother in a deep coma, after a stroke. The hospital staff told her that if her mother had been brought in any later, she could have died. In fact, she made a full recovery.

The majority of the people who appeared were still living in this dimension, and something or somebody was bringing to my notice that they needed help. This is another such case.

I was speaking to a friend on the phone when I saw the face of a patient on a nearby wall. I was not particularly perturbed as I had only seen her two days ago and she had seemed to be quite well. However, I decided to call her and find out if she needed any help. There was no answer. I then contacted a friend who lived nearby, and she told me that my patient had fallen down and broken her leg only hours before I had called, and that she was at the moment being attended to at the local hospital.

'It's strange,' she said, 'I've only just walked through the door. I came back home to leave a message for my son when he arrives home from school.'

It was not in the least strange to me. The moment had obviously been planned by someone.

I saw a child's face appear on the wall behind the television, and immediately recognized it as the grandaughter of a patient. The child was crying. This worried me so much that I spent nearly all day trying to contact the grandmother. When I eventually caught up with her, she told me that her daughter had left home, and that she was looking after her two children. She had been unable to console the youngest child, who had been crying all day.

'Betty,' she said, 'you must ask your spirit friends to send my daughter home. We are all distraught.'

I promised her that I would do all that I could, and spent an hour in my healing room that night asking for help.

Four days later the young mother returned, and when the grandmother told her that her young daughter's distressed face had appeared on my wall, she broke down and cried. She immediately called and thanked me. 'Now that I know someone is watching over me, I feel that I can manage.' she said. That knowledge gave her the strength she needed, and enabled the family to stay together.

Because of my research in this field I had begun teaching the principles of mind projection, with simple exercises. I had long ago realized that nothing is ever wasted. The faces that had appeared on the wall had shown me the possibility of mind projection, and I felt that if the spirits could do it, then so could I.

I began to use remote viewing more frequently. For instance, when I was asked to give absent healing, I asked if I could use this method as part of the process of healing, so that I could get closer to the patient. No one refused; in fact they were delighted by the idea and, through remote viewing, I was able to solve a few mysteries.

On one particular occasion, I visited the home of a child who was suffering severe asthma attacks. The medical profession had apparently been unable to help and the parents were desperate with worry. Using remote viewing, I gained the impression, when I entered the house, that the air was full of minute particles of dust – so much so that I began to sneeze myself. I mentally scanned the house and found myself in the child's bedroom. Something directed me to a vacuum cleaner standing in the corner of the room, and I knew instinctively that this was the cause of the problem.

I called the child's father and told him my fears, asking him to remove the cleaner from the bedroom. He promised to look into the matter. He phoned me later in the day to tell me that the cleaner had a fault, and that the dirt was being distributed around the house, and not into the dust bag. This was rectified, and two weeks later the child was free of symptoms.

No doubt the fault would have been found in time, but the child's suffering would have been extended.

Images are projected in many forms. I have been asked, time and time again, why certain people show themselves in uniforms now that they have left this world and are living in a spiritual environment. One of the reasons is that their family and friends will recognize them as they were – and it was also probably a time in their lives when they were happy. Spirits show themselves in what used to be their favourite clothes, and this seems to make sense to the recipients of the messages. They recognize that the clothes resemble the happiest time in the life of that person.

Spirits also project images of animals, usually pets who have been long gone, but never forgotten. These images have also been shown to me during survival evidence.

On one occasion I was shown four different breeds of dog. Before I could pass on this information, my sitter asked me if I could hear dogs barking. Because of the love that had existed between her and her animals, she had immediately linked in with them. I was able to give her detailed descriptions of the dogs, and told her that two were Labradors that had belonged to her sister. And the Jack Russell, Yorkshire terrier and Dachshund had belonged to her. She was absolutely delighted. The knowledge that her beloved pets were still existing somewhere, and had loved her enough to show themselves to her once more, changed her life.

She confided that she had become ill because of her negativity, and wondered every day why she still kept going. Now she felt that the love that she had shared with her animals would be there forever, and that one day she would be reunited with them.

It has often caused great amusement when I have described the actions of some of the animals I was being shown. The owners have always recognized the antics of their beloved pet. I remember one lovely wire-haired terrier in particular.

My sitter was a young lady called Gillian. I was giving her survival evidence when I saw the spirit of a little terrier dancing around in rings on the floor. I began to laugh, because he was giving such a marvellous performance. I asked Gillian if she had owned a terrier, and described his antics to her.

'Oh no, I can't believe it!' she exclaimed. 'That is Toby.' She explained that she had bought him from a dog's home, and from the time she had taken him home he had never stopped performing. Smiling through her tears, she said, 'Everyone loved him. I know I'll never own another Toby as long as I live. I'm so thrilled that he's still with me.'

'Do you think he might have belonged to a circus at one time?' I asked.

'He must have done,' she declared. 'Where else would he have learned to act like that.'

More and more, during my relaxation periods, spirit children were materializing. Several of them were ex-patients, whose lives had been eased with healing when they were terminally ill. Others I did not recognize. They all asked me to contact their parents. Sometimes I had to hunt through old diaries to obtain the telephone numbers or addresses of those I had treated so that I could pass on messages from the children. Here are some of their stories.

Janey had been six years old when she had died of a brain tumour. When she appeared, she asked me to tell her mother that she and Auntie Lucy sent her lots of hugs and kisses. Also, that she had been reunited with her pet budgerigar. I am always concerned when I contact the parents of a child who has died, as it will bring back the heartbreak they suffered. Nevertheless, I do not feel that I have a choice. I rang Janey's parents. Her mother answered the phone, and when I told her that Janey had been to see me, she was speechless for a few moments. Then she said, 'Did she have a message for me?'

I passed on the messages. As I did so I could hear her crying softly, and apologised for upsetting her.

'I'm not upset. I think it's wonderful.' She hesitated. 'I had no idea that this sort of thing could happen.'

'Was Lucy your sister?' I asked.

'Yes,' she replied, 'my older sister. She died two years before Janey.'

'What about the budgie?' I asked. 'When did he die?'

'Six months before Janey,' she said. 'Betty, I believe she has come through to you to prove that she's survived. You see, her father doesn't believe in life after death, and I've been very worried about him. He cannot accept that his daughter has gone. Perhaps this will be the turning point for him.'

'There is always a good reason why these things happen.' I told her.

We talked for a while. She told me how grateful she was for passing on Janey's message, and when I put the phone down I knew it had all been worth the effort.

I met Janey's mother a year later and she told me that my call had changed her husband's attitude so much that he now regularly attended his local church.

The next story is about about called Jack, who had died of cancer at the age of fifteen.

When Jack appeared, he asked me to tell his mother to get on with her life. He told me that since his death she had given up all her activities, and that this was making him very unhappy. He also wanted her to give his bedroom to Vicky, her sister, as she needed somewhere private to study for her A levels.

Once again I searched through my diaries. I found the address, but there was no phone number. Using the address I tried to find the number but was told that it was ex-directory. I wrote the messages down and sent them with a letter to Jack's mother. And in the light of Jack's message I decided to give her some absent healing. A week later I received a very moving letter from his father. He told me that his wife had been unable to cry since Jack's death and, consequently, had been ill most of the time. Since receiving my letter, she had not been able to stop crying.

'I know she will recover now,' he wrote, 'because there is no way you could have known about Vicky's problems. Or my wife's health. We have to believe that Jack has survived now. We all thank you from the bottom of our hearts.'

There was little I could do about the children I did not recognize, other than give them masses of love. I know they were aware of it, because one day, when I was giving survival evidence to a mother who had lost her son, he suddenly said, 'When you're not here Betty looks after us.' His mother asked me what he meant, and I had to tell her that I didn't know but that I would try to find out. A few minutes later the child told me, 'You saw me the other day.' It was then I remembered a little boy who had materialized a few days ago. I had not recognized him, but had given him a mental hug. When I told his mother the story she asked me to describe him, which I did, adding, 'He had a small scar on his lip.' It was this small detail that finally convinced her that I had seen him.

When parents lose a child the loss stays with them forever. They are destroyed by the thought that they will never again be able to hold them. When I have pointed out that they can communicate telepathically with their children, and that no thought is ever wasted, it changes their whole outlook. Unless the parent is psychic they probably will never be able to see their child again, at least not until they join them in the other dimension. But they can have telepathic conversations with them. The thought is the deed. By simply looking at a photograph of the child, you are immediately in touch with them. Women are definitely better at this kind of communication than men, who seem to surround themselves with all kinds of 'so called' rational obstructions. It is only when you 'know' that you can do something, that it works. Like swimming and riding a bicycle, once you have done it you know that you will always be able to do it. It can be frustrating, at first, not knowing whether the message is getting through or not. Eventually, however, you will begin to have a gut feeling about it, and possibly find thoughts in your head that you know you haven't put there. Let me explain.

A young mother had lost her daughter in a car crash. When she came to see me she was totally distraught, until I taught her how to speak to her daughter telepathically. About three weeks later she came to see me again, and told me that she had been having a conversation with her daughter every night, before going to bed. Her husband had told her not to do this, but she ignored him, telling him that it was the only time she felt at peace. After a week of these 'conversations' with her little girl, she heard the child call her. 'I distinctly heard her say, "Mummy!"' she said. Her eyes glowing, she went on. 'In the morning, I went into her room and there, sitting in the middle of her bed, was her favourite teddy. When she died, I put all her toys, including the teddy, into a cupboard.'

'Could your husband have put it there?' I asked.

'No,' she replied. 'He knows that it would have upset me.'

'How did he respond when you told him what had happened?'

'He just wouldn't believe me,' she replied. 'But there's something else. When I looked into her bedroom the following morning, her recorder was on the bed beside the teddy.' She laughed delightedly, 'You see, she is answering me in her own way.' The little girl continued to communicate in small ways for some time, but her mother was already convinced by these two experiences, and this enabled her to pick up the pieces and live again. Later, she had another daughter.

Some parents try to obtain proof by giving their children tasks to perform. In my opinion they should not do this. If the children can give proof, they will do so. If not, one just has to have masses of faith. There are parents now who communicate regularly with the children they have lost, and they have told me that they can 'feel' when their children are around. As one woman said, 'I feel an excitement when my son is near me; it feels like bubbles rising all around me.' She is quite right and has become aware of the energy that the children bring with them.

During my first two years as a medium I would think, every night when I went to bed, of the heart-rending stories I had heard during the day. I did not think that I could cope with so much sorrow. There was also laughter, of course, but it is the sad stories that stay with you. I gave absent healing, twice a day, to everyone who had visited me and to those seeking help in other ways. I admit to feeling angry when I was unable to help someone who was terminally ill. This anger was the only way I could deal with it at the time. I used to ask for the impossible, and I knew it, but I still asked. Sometimes my prayers were answered and it was this that helped me get up in the morning and start all over again.

I don't think people are aware of the sacrifices that healers and mediums have to make. I was still trying to have a normal life, to go out with my friends and have fun, but it was becoming impossible. There was just not enough time. I had to make my career my life, or I would only have been doing half a job. It is only enthusiasm and hard work that give results, and in this respect mediumship is no different to any other career. Where it differs from other careers – at least until you have made a name for yourself – is the fact that it is difficult to share with others. I was extremely careful during the first two years not to discuss my work with anyone other than my clientele and close family and friends. Times have changed, and the paranormal is now being discussed openly on television and in the media in general. I hope that one day there will be television programmes teaching families how to heal within the home. It is quite extraordinary how many families do not touch and hug each other every day. Touching is a way of passing on the energy of pure love, and that is what healing is. It is totally unlike any other kind of love. It is a chemistry that comes from the soul and that is why lovers feel and look incredibly healthy. Even when they are not having a sexual relationship, they still cannot keep their hands off each other. No matter how old you are, being in love can take years off you, and conversely, when the love affair ends it can put years on you. Remember to touch and heal every day, and in doing so you will be reversing the negative energies in your home.

It is wonderful to receive survival evidence, and to know that someone we have lost still cares about us. But how much love and care did we give them whilst they were still alive? In my work I have seen grown men and women distraught with guilt when their late parents communicate with them. They have told me that, although they had loved them, there never seemed to be time to visit them as often as they would have liked. It is very difficult, when one has a family to bring up, or a taxing career, to find the time. But old people need that loving energy more than the young, and it would extend their lives.

Many of my patients believed they had touched the source of that pure love when they experienced a Near Death Experience or NDE – and I will describe this in the next chapter.

CHAPTER ELEVEN

I AM VERY GRATEFUL TO THOSE PATIENTS who shared their NDEs with me, for teaching me so much about the process of dying, and for confirming my theories about the survival of the mind.

John was an extremely handsome, ambitious man in his early fifties. Because he had asked for healing to rejuvenate his cells, I assumed that he had studied cell therapy. But when I asked him if this was so, he laughed and said, 'You must be joking. I don't know anything about it.'

'So why did you specifically mention the rejuvenation of cells?' I asked.

'Because that is what I was taught when I died,' he replied, and jokingly suggested that I hadn't realized he was a spirit entity.

'If I tell you my story,' he said, 'you probably won't believe me.'

'Try me,' I suggested.

'Well,' he began, 'two years ago, I had a heart attack. The pain was so excruciating that I lost consciousness. What happened after that was incredible. I was spinning around in space and although I knew I was looking for something, I didn't know what it was.' He sighed, and continued. 'Not that it mattered, because I was so relieved at being free from pain. The next thing I remember was spinning toward a black hole.' He shuddered. 'I was frightened and tried to draw back from it, but I was propelled into it. I didn't remember anything else until I saw a bright light so dazzling that I had to close my eyes. Then I noticed a man in the distance. He looked very strange, but as I got closer I could see that his image was distorted because he was standing behind a transparent wall.'

I suggested that this was probably an energy screen, and John agreed. Then he continued with his story.

'The man spoke to me, and told me to stay where I was,' he grinned. 'As I had no control over my movements I didn't have much choice.'

'Then what happened?' I asked, anxious to hear the rest of the story.

'Well,' John went on, 'the wall disappeared, and I found myself standing in a circle of light. At first the light was sunflower yellow, then it turned into all the colours of the rainbow. I couldn't understand what was happening. And then I saw a Being of Light walking toward me.'

'Why do you say it was a Being of Light?' I asked.

'Because the light was coming from within his body,' he replied.

I asked him how he had felt at this point, and whether he thought the Being was Jesus.

'All I could feel was Love,' John said. 'Not the kind of love you have for another human being, this was different. It was all embracing. I've never felt anything like it in my life.' He thought for a moment, and then he said, 'I have wondered since whether it was Jesus, but I just don't know. I'm not a religious man so I have never had any preconceived idea of what Jesus would look like. Anyway, the Light was so bright it would have been difficult for me to distinguish any features. All I can tell you is that I didn't want him to leave.'

I wanted to hear more, 'Did he say anything to you?' I asked.

'No,' John smiled, 'he was walking toward me then he disappeared. The next thing I knew I was looking down on my body. I was lying on what looked like an operating table and there were a lot of people standing around me. Then I was back in my body.' He grimaced. 'And the pain was back.'

I smiled at him, and I said, 'But what about the rejuvenation of cells? Where did that come from?'

'When I eventually recovered from my heart attack, I knew

that I had to seek out someone who could revitalize my cells. And that's why I am here. That's the most cranky part of this story.' Holding his head in his hands, he said, 'Where did I get this information? Do you think I'm crazy?'

'No, I don't. This Being of Light was obviously communicating with you telepathically, and has impressed upon you that you must seek help in this way to keep yourself healthy. I think you are also being warned not to continue living life in the fast lane.'

'Don't worry,' he said, 'that experience has taught me a great deal. There's more to life than working ourselves to death for material gain. I spend more time with my family now, and we are all happier for it.' Looking at me intently, he said, 'You know, I have completely lost my fear of death, and I feel free to live.'

I was fascinated by John's NDE, especially by the first part, when he was drawn into the black hole and then spun into the light. It was very similar to the stories I had heard when listening to survival evidence – the difference being that they had not returned. Through them I had also heard of the Being of Light, and of the Love that came from this person. I had wondered occasionally whether this was one person or whether there many Beings of Light, and was to find out when a young lady called Celia came to see me.

Celia told me her story whilst I was giving her healing.

'I was at work one day,' she said, 'when I suddenly felt very ill. I remember falling, and then suddenly I was being lifted in the air. My memory of that part is very hazy. Then I heard voices, and saw all these people standing around me. The light was so bright around them that I couldn't see their faces, but for some reason I wasn't frightened. Then they vanished and there was only one person left. I knew it was a man, but the light around him was so brilliant it blinded me. He put his hand on my arm, and said, "You will remember this." Then I woke up in a hospital bed.' She had a wonderful smile on her face, when she said, 'I will never forget him.'

'What was it about him that you'll never forget?' I asked.

'The Love,' she answered. 'I can still feel the Love that was given to me, and I try to pass some of it on to others.'

I asked her the same question that I had asked John. 'Do you think there is only one Being of Light?'

She thought for a while and then answered, 'I did see others who were similar, but they didn't seem to have the power of the man who touched me.'

It was all very intriguing. From these two accounts it would seem that there is a group of these Beings but only one all powerful leader.

Mary arrived on my doorstep one day and asked if I would see her. I explained that I was very busy but I would give her an appointment. She explained that she had to return to America the next day; the reason that she had left the visit so late was because she had only just heard about me from a friend. She said she had to talk to me. I invited her in, and promised to fit her into my schedule if she didn't mind waiting. I was able to speak to her an hour later.

'I don't know whether you're going to believe this story or not,' she told me, 'but I just had to tell someone, and my friend gave me your name.' Looking slightly agitated, she continued. 'Six months ago, whilst going through a divorce, I had a heart attack. The pain was dreadful. But what is etched on my mind, and will be for the rest of my life, is what happened to me when I lost consciousness. I was travelling through a tunnel at great speed and I remember thinking "this is the mainstream".'

'Were you in darkness, or was it light?' I asked.

'I don't remember, but when I reached the other end of the tunnel it was bright sunlight, and I found myself standing on the banks of a great river.' She hesitated, 'Sorry, I'm trying to give you a clear picture.' I told her to take her time.

'There were people standing on the other side of the river but I couldn't recognize any of them as they were too far away. Then, suddenly, I was surrounded by members of my late family and by my parents. They were all trying to speak to me at the same time. Then there was silence, and my mother hugged me and said, "We have only been given permission to cross the river for a short while."' Mary's face was wreathed in smiles as she spoke about her mother. 'I was able to hug her and kiss her. It was incredible.' As she paused, I asked whether her mother had given her a message. When she answered, she had a faraway look in her eyes, as though she was reliving her experience. 'My mother told me that I couldn't stay, that I had to go back,' she said. 'I was devastated. We'd only just found each other again. I asked why I had to return, and she smiled, and stroked my face. "It isn't time yet," she told me. The rest is all a bit vague. I don't remember how we parted, or going back through the tunnel, and then I was looking into the eyes of my friend, who said, "Mary, you've been far away, haven't you?" I nodded and fell asleep.'

'It's a wonderful story,' I said, 'and you obviously have no qualms about accepting the fact that you have been "out of this world". What is it that you can't accept?'

Mary smiled. 'You'll probably think I'm silly, but I just can't understand why, having made the journey, I wasn't allowed to stay. I've never been a spiritual soul, and I'm not making any impact on this planet, so why did I have to come back?'

'Do you mean to say that you still haven't worked it out for yourself?' I asked.

'No, that's why I'm here,' she answered.

'Well, it's perfectly obvious to me,' I said. 'The fact that you were not religious or spiritually inclined made you a perfect candidate. You've been describing your experience to friends and, perhaps, to others who may be interested.' Mary nodded. 'Don't you see,' I went on. 'You're spreading the "word", and people believe you simply because you are such an unlikely candidate.'

'What do you mean? What is the "word",' she asked.

'That there is life after death,' I replied.

Mary looked at me in disbelief. 'I hadn't thought of it like that. I don't believe it, I've been conned.'

I laughed. 'Yes! But in the nicest possible way. To bring about peace, and understanding of an afterlife, the powers that be will use every avenue open to them.'

This information had been given to me by my guru. This is what he said:

There will be great changes in the next twenty years. Those who have never before envisaged a life after death will be given the experience, so that they may return and teach others. We are already using every avenue open to us to bring about a transformation in your world, and I will give you the reason for these actions.

When the soul/mind leaves the sheath/body we have to take everyone back through their earth life so that they will understand how every thought and deed has affected others. This is the so-called Heaven or Hell. They are never alone when this is happening, and although there is redemption for the crimes – of any kind – that they have committed against life, in the end they are alone and must atone for these actions. It is traumatic for all of us who are involved in this work and we are, therefore, taking every opportunity to educate and give everyone the chance to evaluate their lives before they arrive here.

Most of the people who return to your world to tell their story would never have returned to their sheath were it not for our actions. As I have said, we are taking every opportunity that is given to us.

This message was given to me in 1981, and I have received confirmation of his words many times through stories of near death experiences. It is most inspiring to know that people have lost their fear of being ridiculed.

So many people lead empty fruitless lives which have been changed by a Near Death Experience. Len was one such person.

'I never cared much for other people,' he told me. 'And I hated children, which is why I never married. I'd lived alone all my life and although it was lonely at times, it never really bothered me.' He stopped, and stared ahead, as though trying to conjure up a picture in his mind, and then he continued with his story. 'That is, until I went into a coma. I have diabetes,' he explained, then frowned. 'You know, if someone else told me this story, I would never have believed them.' There was another pause. Intrigued, I urged him to continue. 'I went to heaven,' he said. 'Me! Can you believe it! I went to heaven. I thought only Christians went to heaven.'

'How did you get there?' I asked.

'God only knows!' he said.

Pursuing my line of questioning, I asked, 'Did you go into a tunnel, and reach the light?'

'No,' he said. 'Nothing like that. I just arrived.' His face lit up as he spoke. 'There was a golden glow all around me, as though there were several suns. Then rays of all different colours danced around me. I was so happy.' He sat smiling to himself for a few minutes, and then said, 'But I had to pay for it.' I asked what he meant. 'Well, the next bit was horrible. I was sitting in a hall and my whole life was being shown on a big screen. Although it was going very fast, I could feel every hurt that I had caused to other people in my life, and when it was over I was told I had to repay a debt to society.' Shaking his head, he said, 'I didn't understand how I could do that. Then I woke up in hospital. When I recovered I found that I had completely changed. I have plenty of friends now and I married a woman with a grown-up family and give our grandchildren all the love I can. Only now can I see how barren my life was before I went to heaven.'

'When you were there, did you feel surrounded by love?'

'Yes I did, though before I died I hadn't known what it felt like. I do now.' He laughed. 'You must think I'm mad.'

'Not at all,' I said, 'I've heard too many Near Death Experiences to think that. In fact, it has taught me a lot.'

'Is that what it's called?' he asked.

'Yes. You see, you don't actually cross the line into another dimension, so it is a near death.'

Now it was his turn to be intrigued, and he plied me with questions until it was time for him to leave.

What fascinated me most about these NDEs was the fact that all the stories were so different. Although the majority of people were drawn into a tunnel in the beginning, they never seemed to end up in the same place at the end of it – although it seemed that the light at the end of the tunnel was common to everyone who travelled through it.

Because I understood energy vortices I could see that it would be natural for the mind to spin and turn into a vortex, giving the impression that one was travelling through a tunnel.

I understand from my spiritual teachers that the Universe is indeed a mass of vortices, and that the surge of energy created by these controls the mass.

Emma was a thirty-year-old and had been in a car accident. This was her experience.

'I was standing by the side of the road, and although I could see people looking at a body, I didn't realize that it was mine. I tried to talk to them but it seemed that nobody wanted to listen to me. Then I saw this black hole coming toward me, and I was swallowed up and hurled toward a bright light. When I reached the end of this black hole, my maternal grandmother was there to meet me. We hugged and kissed, and she told me that I had to go back as my mother was so upset.' As she recounted her story, I recognized that same glow on Emma's face, that I had seen on others when they told me about their experiences.

'In my grandmother's hug,' Emma went on, 'I could feel the Love of the Universe. It filled my whole being. I've never felt love like that since.'

'Not even from your mother?' I asked.

'No! My mother would have no knowledge of such a love.' She frowned. 'You see, here on earth, we don't know about that kind of love. It is all forgiving.'

'After your experience, do you think that you can give this kind of love?'

'No! I believe you would have to be free of your body first,' she replied.

'Why?'

She was silent for a few moments, and then she said, faintly, 'Because I know.'

When she left, I felt that Emma had not wanted me to question her any further; the experience had been so sacred to her that she did not want to spoil the magic of it.

I could understand that feeling. Sometimes, when I have tried to share my own spiritual experiences with others and a debate ensues, one feels as though it has been tainted in some way.

An elderly gentleman named Syd visited me one day, and asked if I could cure his arthritis. I said I would try. Whilst I was healing him he told me about his Near Death Experience.

'I went into hospital for a hernia operation,' he said. 'I seemed to be getting on well for the first two days and then, at about nine in the evening, I felt myself being propelled out through my head. I can tell you it felt very strange indeed.' He paused. 'I couldn't feel my body, but a part of me was spinning into a dark tunnel, and I remember thinking that this was death. Then I saw a light ahead, and when I reached it all my family were there waiting for me. A couple of them had been dead for about fifty years.' He propped himself up on the couch, and said, 'Does this sound strange to you? After all, I'm not a medium.'

'No, it doesn't sound strange at all,' I replied.

Settling himself down again he continued with his story. 'My mother, father and two brothers came forward and held out their arms to me. They hugged and kissed me, even my father, and I can't remember seeing him kiss anyone when he was alive. I've never felt so much love in all my life.'

'What happened then?' I asked.

'Well,' he said, 'when they had finished greeting me, I heard a rushing sound, and then they said they had to go. I told them that I was going with them, but my mother said I had to go back.' At this point he began to cry. 'I saw this great river rushing past. They slipped into it and then they were gone. I heard a voice saying that they had entered the slipstream.'

'Do you think it was a river of water, or some other substance?' I asked.

Wiping his eyes, he said, 'That was the strange thing. It looked like a normal river at first, and then it changed into something else, and I found myself standing alone in the middle of a huge field. I heard a voice say, "You see, life is eternal." The next thing I remember is waking up in bed surrounded by doctors and nurses.'

I asked whether he had told them about his experience.

'I tried to,' he said, 'but they didn't take any notice. They probably thought I'd gone off my head.'

'Has it made any difference to your life?'

'Well, I'm not afraid of death any more and, apart from my arthritis, I feel better than I've ever felt in my life.' He chuckled. 'And I look ten years younger – which is quite a bonus.'

'How old are you?' I asked, expecting him to tell me that he was about seventy years old.

'I'll be ninety-four next week,' he said.

When people have a Near Death Experience it seems to have a lifetime effect on them, and is something they never forget. The materialistic side of their personality is replaced with a feeling for nature, and concern for all living things. Most of them become vegetarian because they are unable to come to terms with the killing of any creature. They know how to attain the peace that we are all seeking and, no longer fearing death, embrace life as never before. I think we can all learn from this.

CHAPTER TWELVE

S O MUCH WORK, SO LITTLE TIME. That was my waking thought every day. I was trying to fit in hours of healing, clairvoyance, survival evidence, vitamin and mineral therapy, hypnotherapy and counselling, covering every human and spiritual emotion. There was a never-ending stream of people turning up on the doorstep asking if I could fit them in between appointments.

I longed for the times when I could meditate. Very often this would be well into the early hours of the morning, but I never missed; it was the only way I could revitalize myself and listen to the audible silence from which I was able to extract the spiritual knowledge that had become so important to me. I had seen so much mental and physical suffering over the past years, and I longed to be able to perform a miracle for everyone who asked for help. I often thought of the vision I had seen in the early days of my mediumship, where the multitudes were holding up their arms to a distant figure. There were many days when I felt that the figure must have been me. And, although I knew that the final decision was not mine, I was still left with a feeling of inadequacy if I felt that the physical healing had failed, as it must do from time to time. It was a great comfort to know, though, that the spiritual healing never failed. From the first healing a seed is sown which continues to grow in strength.

My day started at 8 a.m., with meditation and absent healing. There were so many people in this country and around the world who could not possibly visit me, for a number of reasons, and this was the only way I could heal them. I felt duty-bound to give this time to everyone who asked for help. At 9.30 a.m. I saw my first patient of the day and generally worked through to ten or eleven p.m. with perhaps an hour's break at lunch time. The days were long and hard, but whilst I was working time became immaterial, as I constantly switched from one world to another.

But help was at hand. One day, during a break between appointments, I was shown how to set up an energy network around the world. At first the clairvoyant picture I was given looked extremely complicated, but when it was explained it became clear that, in fact, it was simplicity itself. The thought was the deed. All I had to do was mentally slip the name of the person to be healed into the network by projecting the name onto the diagram, and healing would take place. I was told that it would not be necessary for me to think of all the names every day. Once they had been placed in the network, all I had to do was picture the diagram and mentally place my hands upon it and ask for healing, and this would keep the network alive. Obviously I had to enter any new names, but this method saved me so much time. It worked like magic. Over the years I have used my own imagination and updated the network, but the original thought is still there and has been used to heal thousands of people. Someone had obviously become aware of my predicament as far as time was concerned, and I will be forever grateful for the help I received in this way.

My spirit friends were never far away, and when I least expected it, the column of energy would appear in my hall. This gave me an idea. Why not place the image of a patient in the column? Especially when it was blue, because blue is the colour of healing energy. At that time I had a very sick little girl who was visiting me twice a week, and I wanted to try and speed up the healing. First of all, I decided to ask my spirit teachers if this was permissible and when I did not receive an answer, reluctantly dropped the idea. Then the little girl's mother confided that she had been seeing the word 'yes' in her mind for about a week, and did I think it had anything to do with the healing? I was delighted, and told her the story. I also felt relieved that the final decision had been left to the mother. She told me to go ahead with my plan, and within three weeks the little girl was on her way to making a complete recovery. I used this method for those patients who were very sick, and was delighted with the results. These experiments taught me much about the power of the mind.

The results of world-wide healing have been unbelievable. My team, as I call my spirit doctors, have achieved results beyond my wildest dreams.

I understand how difficult it must be for those people who are asked to have faith in absent healing. After all, they have nothing to go on but results. Fortunately, the majority do have faith and stay with this healing process. For those who live in isolated conditions, they have no choice. But their faith has been rewarded.

One such person was Rod, who lived in the outback in Australia. He had a cattle ranch and was on the back of his horse fifteen hours a day. He even ate his snacks on horseback. He wrote to me asking for help; his spine had been damaged through too many falls, and the specialists had told him that he must never ride again. He was in despair, because the ranch was his only source of in-come, and it would take two men to do the work that he got through every day. He simply could not afford to pay two more hands.

He had been told about me by a friend who had visited me in England. As he said in his letter, 'I haven't the faintest idea what this is all about, but please help me.'

I felt so sorry for him that I slipped him into the energy column and the network. Six weeks later I received this letter:

'What can I say! From the beginning I felt a tingling all over my body, then came the heat – which was nothing to do with the weather, I can assure you. I was still in pain a week later, when I felt a punch in my back. I looked around but there was no one there. I thought I had imagined it, and it was then that I realised I was no longer in pain. Three weeks later, I am still free from pain. I don't understand these things but I will be forever grateful. If you need a holiday, come and stay with us.'

A year later Rod was still out of pain.

A mother wrote to me from South Africa, telling me that her sixteen year old daughter was in a coma with an inoperable brain tumour, and begging me to help. Again, I slotted the girl's name into the energy column and the network. Whilst I was giving her healing, a voice told me to contact the mother and tell her that she must get in touch with a certain doctor who would be able to help. I called and gave the doctor's name. She had never heard of him, but said she would make enquiries. She called me hours later to say that she had made contact with him and, after telling him about the message she had received from me, he assured her that he would take the case on himself. He operated, and the young girl made a full recovery.

I have chosen these examples because they show what the world-wide network can achieve. But I admit that I would have been really shaken had I known, many years later, that I would be receiving thousands of letters a week, asking for help.

There were many unexpected requests. I had never been terribly good at geography, and was slightly put out when I began to receive maps from around the world, asking for help in tracing long lost relatives, animals, treasure trove, cars, to name but a few. I really had no time to look at maps, so I had to return the majority of them to their owners. But occasionally I would be looking at a particular map and receive a spirit message, and in those circumstances I felt duty bound to do something about it.

One request was from a woman who lived in a very isolated part of South Africa. She asked me to help her with the wild dogs that surrounded her house every night, looking for food. I had already helped another gentleman with the same problem, by pin-pointing a place on the map and mentally asking the dogs to move of their own accord. They had gone, and when the man passed their new home much later he found that it was an area where there was an abundance of food and water. So I used the same method, hoping for the same results, but for three months nothing happened. By this time the woman was desperate. I tried every spiritual means available to me to bring about a successful result. Then I received this letter:

'The barking and howling from the dogs was so bad one night that it was impossible to sleep. I got out of bed, and walked over to the window. A large dog stood on the top of a hill nearby, and it was howling. I couldn't understand why it was alone, and stood watching it for some time. Then the other dogs began to move away from the house, and one by one formed a line and began walking up the hill. When they had all joined the lone dog on the hill, they disappeared, and I haven't seen them since. Do you think it was a spirit leading them to a better place?'

I don't know whether the lone dog was a spirit or not, but she was never bothered with the wild dogs again. I like to think that one of their own kind had been chosen to lead them to a land of plenty, where they would never be hungry again. Perhaps it did.

Then there was the case of the missing relative – the daughter of a Spanish business man who was dying, and who wished to be reunited with her before the end. This family could give me no clues at all as to the probable whereabouts of his daughter. Having lived in Spain for some years I was more familiar with the Spanish maps than I had been with others I had received. However, when the time came to study it, I drew a blank. Then one night I dreamt that I was on a rock and was surrounded by apes. When I awoke I looked at the map again and my eyes travelled down towards Gibraltar, of course, the rock with the apes. I called the girl's mother and she told me that she would send one of her brothers to find her. A week later the daughter was reunited with her father, and he died a happy man.

Map Dowsing

Map dowsing has been particularly helpful when friends have been undecided about the location of a new house. I have been able to scan the map and pin-point the most suitable area for their needs. At the same time, I found that I could also detect any structural defects within the properties. This was so successful that I began to look for defects in the grounds and surrounding properties. I was given information about damp courses and sinking below the surface, damage to the roofs, and a host of otherwise hidden defects. There were many times when I detected a certain sickness about the house. Then I would suggest that the would-be owner look into the history of the place. Sometimes the sickness was apparent, such as when I saw an underground stream directly beneath the house; this is a known cause for many health problems.

It is possible to heal properties, and I did this on a number of occasions. In nearly every case I was given a mental picture of the surrounding land and garden, which showed up possible future complications and disputes. For instance, on several occasions I was given a view of rubbish dumps outside the perimeter of the gardens. When investigated, my findings were found to be correct.

Another instance which saved an enormous amount of problems was when I received a mental picture of two dogs bounding through a broken fence that divided the gardens. I saw the dogs romping around and generally going berserk. When I reported this scene to the friend who had asked me to scan the property, she immediately visited the house and saw the scene for herself. She told me later that the fence had been the last job on their list, but after seeing the neighbours' dogs wrecking the garden, it went to the top of the list and she had it fixed before they moved in. There is no doubt that this action prevented a possible dispute, which is the last thing anyone needs when moving to a new neighbourhood.

In another garden I saw that the double-barred front gate was hanging off its hinges. When I reported back, I was told that the gate was going to be scrapped and not replaced as it would be so much easier to drive directly into the garage. I urged the new owners to change their minds and replace the gate. When they asked why, I told them that I had been given a scene of the lane leading up to the house which was at the end of a cul-de-sac, and could see innumerable cars backing into their drive to turn around – which was probably the reason for the double gate having been put there in the first place. Unfortunately, when they bought the house, they stayed with their decision and did not replace the gate. Their lives were made a misery as car after car reversed into their drive. This caused endless quarrels with their new neighbours and visitors, and in the end they replaced the gate. It caused them a lot of inconvenience but their peace of mind was restored.

The worst thing about moving house is that there are usually so many hidden defects in the new property and surrounding area that don't show up until one has actually moved in. Even though it is possible to ask around, there is no way that other people are going to run down the area because they usually have a vested interest in it. There are also so many cover-ups by the people selling the property, which is understandable but not very spiritual.

The only time my map reading scanning went slightly awry was when I tried to find the likely destination for Michael Bentine's new home. At the time I was living in Sutton, and Michael was living in Epsom, both places in Surrey. Looking at the map, I pointed to a place in Sussex, and said, 'That's where you're going to live.' He looked somewhat mystified by this suggestion, but was too polite to say anything. I wasn't very happy either, as I spent quite a lot of weekends with Michael and his wife. About a year later, I moved to Sussex, only ten minutes drive from the location I had given Michael. When I had looked at the map I had had no intention of moving; as far as I was concerned I was going to spend the rest of my life in Surrey. Obviously, someone else had other ideas, which confirmed my belief that there was more to scanning than merely projecting mind energy.

I do not believe that it is possible to be successful in this field without spiritual help. When we concentrate on something outside of ourselves, the pressure is taken away from the body and the mind expands and links up with higher minds. It is from this source that we are given the ability to help others. I am convinced that we are only as good as our spiritual teachers and helpers.

If you are thinking of moving perhaps you would like to try this exercise: write the address of the possible new home on a piece of paper, close your eyes and place your hands on the paper. Do not try to bring images to mind, just allow your thoughts to centre on the address. Within minutes, you should get feedback and gut feelings about the place and, if you are lucky, images will appear in your mind.

But do not worry if they don't, because the gut feeling should be enough to help you make up your mind.

Mind Dowsing

Mind dowsing can be used for a number of things, but the greatest benefit is when you are aware that someone is helping you. This, of course, can only be judged by results, but it is worthwhile using this method to ask questions that you are unable to answer yourself. You will be surprised at the answers you receive. This can happen in several ways. If you ask a question before going to sleep, it is more than likely that you will wake with the answer in the morning. Or an answer will come into your mind so powerfully that you can almost see it. One young lady I knew used the pockets of a shoe holder to 'post' her questions, then ran her hands over it and asked for help. At odd times during the day she told me she could feel the answers being slotted into her mind. This practice gradually gave her the confidence to take responsibility for her own life. She had been too dependent on others, and this had caused her great unhappiness.

Whatever method you use, make it a regular habit, because sooner or later a spiritual helper will become aware of your need and you will receive help.

It is also an admirable way of becoming independent, and that will also give you the freedom of thought, word and deed.

There can be nothing worse than total dependency, as this eventually leads to mental and physical anguish. I know, because I have too often seen the results. People very often give up and lean on others because it is the easy way out, but in the end, their paths are far from easy. If you start now, I think you will be surprised at the happiness and success you can achieve.

CHAPTER THIRTEEN

DEPENDENCY! I HAD NO IDEA when I began healing how many people suffered from the effects of this problem. The ailments ranged from simple headaches to life threatening diseases. Suicide was often mentioned as the only way out. Parents who doted on their offspring often left them unable to think for themselves. Married women found themselves in an unenviable position when their partners died, unable to sort out insurance claims or even complete a simple task like filling their car with petrol. It was worse for the couples who had locked everyone out of their lives and lived only for each other. When their partner died it was a total catastrophe; they were left with no friends or family to comfort them. Men who had been totally reliant on partners found it impossible to function alone, and in some cases, complicated their lives by marrying again only to find out that the wrong kind of marriage can lead to even worse disasters. And parents can be bitterly disappointed when they find that they are becoming a burden to their children.

The majority of the people who visited me with these problems were helped through survival evidence, clairvoyance and healing, but I always insisted that they thought about the situation for some time before making a decision for their future. And it had to be their decision. There was no point in ridding themselves of one kind of dependency and acquiring another. The following are some of the cases that I was involved with.

Maxine had been happily married for thirty-six years, and had enjoyed a luxurious lifestyle throughout that time. Her every wish was granted.

Her husband died suddenly of a heart attack, and in the ensuing year she lost everything. When she came to see me she was on the verge of suicide. Then her husband contacted me and gave her this message.

'I love you, Maxine. I always will, and I am so sorry for the predicament in which you now find yourself. Although I tried to protect you I never thought that you might be left alone, and now it has happened I can only help you from afar. I can see now that I have done you a great injustice. I will find you somewhere to live, and then you must use your own in-built survival kit.'

Maxine asked me what he meant by the last remark. I told her that the only personal survival kit that I knew of was the mind.

I gave her healing and, as I did so, I had a vision of a small village street, and halfway up the street, I saw a small house. Then I was shown the interior of this small house. I described what I could see, and she asked me if the village had a name. I could not give her this, but later in the healing I was given the name, and passed it on. I told her that I thought it was her husband who was projecting these pictures to me.

Three weeks later Maxine visited me again. She told me that she hadn't been able to locate that particular house but had loved the village, which was only about six miles from where she lived.

Her home had already been sold, and she was waiting to have a meeting with her husband's accountants. At this time she had no idea what she was worth.

Six months later, Maxine was able to look at the houses available in the village and bought the one whose interior matched the description I had given her.

When I last saw her she was working as a photographer's assistant. She was loving every minute of it, and told me that for the first time in her life, she felt fulfilled.

The transformation in all those who eventually chose to take responsibility for their lives was a sight to behold. Their eyes shone, they looked like the free spirits they were, and one could feel the happiness they exuded. None of them had an easy transition, but they were determined to achieve the independence they so desired, and they won.

Leela was eighteen years old. Her parents had protected her all her life, never allowing her to go out alone or with other girls of her own age. Her mother first brought her to me for healing, because she had injured her foot whilst walking. Whenever I asked Leela a question, her mother would answer it for her. In fact the girl did not even try to answer, as she obviously thought the effort would be wasted. I felt the frustration within her, but could do nothing in her mother's presence. However, the following week she came alone, and I was able to talk to her for some time. She was very intelligent, and confided that she was at a loss as to know how to handle her mother. 'I don't think she believes I have a mind of my own,' she said.

Whilst she was speaking, her late grandmother contacted me. After checking whether Leela would be happy to receive survival evidence, I passed on the message.

'Your mother has never changed. She was just the same when she was your age. I loved her dearly, but spent most of my life opposing her. She has to be in control all the time and you must put your foot down – in fact you should have done so a long time ago.' Leela's grandmother then gave her many family names, past and present, and talked about the problems that some of them were experiencing at that moment. She finished by telling the young woman that she must insist on having a life of her own. Leela told me that this would be very difficult; her father backed her mother all the way, for his own peace of mind.

However, the message from her grandmother had given Leela so much strength that her mother finally gave in and allowed her more freedom. It was to be two years before her mother refrained from interfering in her conversations, but she won in the end.

I think this story is a salutary lesson for possessive parents. Although they mean well, their actions can cause a great deal of harm. Learning to let go is difficult, but it's a lesson we all have to learn. We all have to let go in differing circumstances throughout out lives.

Barbara had been having an affair with a married man for twelve years. From the beginning, she had begged him to tell his wife so that Barbara would not, as she put it, 'be crawling behind bushes all my life'. He refused, making his children the excuse for not owning up. Barbara told me that although she was still very much in love with the man, she had told him their relationship was over. Since then, he had pestered her at home and at work, sending flowers daily, and making threats of suicide if she did not return to him.

She had been receiving healing from me for four weeks. During that time we had talked about the problems that they both faced. Her lover was obviously more dependent on her than she had realized. But as he still maintained that he could not leave his wife, Barbara had no choice but to seek a life elsewhere, and although she had come to terms with this fact, she still worried that she would cause his suicide. Then her late father contacted her through me.

'You deserve better,' he told her.

Barbara burst into tears. 'Tell her she must go to Tilly,' he said.

'Tilly lives in Austria,' Barbara replied. 'I can't live there.'

Her father spoke again. 'Move right away. It's the only solution.'

He then talked to her about her family, and finished with the words, 'Don't contact him ever again.'

Barbara was beside herself, and asked how she could possibly live in Austria. I suggested that her father was probably trying to point out that it would be a good idea for her to move away for a time. It was patently obvious that her lover would never leave her alone.

Later, I heard that she had gone to Austria for a holiday, had fallen in love and married a friend of Tilly's, and had made her home in that country.

Her lover, on the other hand, became seriously depressed and his wife left him, taking the children with her.

Although others may judge those who indulge in extra-marital affairs, it is, nevertheless, a kind of marriage, and letting go can be very distressing to both parties. If there is a dependency problem on either side, the only cure is for one of them to move away.

I first became aware that as a medium and healer I had no right to judge others when, during a particularly draining time listening to a wife slandering her husband, I began to feel desperately sorry for the husband. My thoughts were immediately interrupted by a voice saying, 'Judge not, lest ye be judged.'

Later, when I looked at my own life, I realized that one cannot and should not judge others. No one can ever know the full story of why we take certain actions in our lives. Outsiders can only see the effect they have but, in practically every case, there are extenuating circumstances. In my own life and in my work I have seen and heard the inside stories, and some of them are truly mind shattering. Very often it is the guilty party who receives the most sympathy. It is better to put everything behind you and begin again, but this is hard especially when memories come crowding in when you least expect them.

Life is not easy, and there are no quick answers to all the problems we have to face. But I do believe that spirituality gives us the strength to carry on, and the knowledge that our loved ones still live – and try to contact us from time to time with messages of love and hope – sustains us when things are bad.

Everyone too, has a spiritual minder, but this does not necessarily mean that they will help you over every hurdle. The more hurdles we are seen to jump by ourselves, the more help we will receive when the matter is truly urgent. It is all a question of progression, and of showing how much spiritual stamina we have.

I have spoken to hundreds of people who are approaching old age, and they all have stories to tell which are fascinating. Some of them are also heart-rending, especially when they talk about the way their lives have been changed because they can no longer look after themselves. The happiest are those who have been given small flats with wardens to attend to them if they are ill. The unhappiest are those who, for one reason or another, have to live with their children. No matter how much love there is in the family, they hate the dependency. I do not think town planners give enough thought to warden operated flats. There should be more of them, especially as people are now living well into their eighties and nineties.

The next story is of one such person.

Nell was a sprightly eighty-eight-year-old, great grandmother. Her daughter brought her to me as she was suffering from severe arthritis. They argued all through the healing and eventually I asked them to stop. Then Nell's late husband contacted me, and said, 'Will you tell them that I love them both.' I passed this message on.

Nell began to cry, and then she said, 'If he was still here I'd be living in my own home.'

'Was your husband's name Len?' I asked.

Nell nodded. 'Yes.'

'Well, Len is telling me that your troubles will soon be over.'

'You mean I'm going to die?' she asked.

'No not at all,' I replied. 'It seems that he is going to sort things out for you, and as he is smiling, I assume it is going to be a happy ending.'

Nell's daughter had been quietly listening to our conversation. At this point she said, 'Betty, Mum has to live with us. She has no money of her own.'

I smiled. 'I've given these sort of messages so often that I really think you should believe your Dad. They can sort things out better than we can because they have an overall view of the whole situation.'

I saw Nell and her daughter every week for about six weeks. Although nothing more was said about their situation or the message they had received, their relationship seemed to be easier.

A year later, the daughter visited me alone. When I asked her where Nell was she told me that her mother was sharing a flat with a friend. I asked how this had happened.

'Well,' she said, 'do you remember giving me that message from my Dad?'

'Yes.'

'Mum repeated it to an old friend, and laughingly said that she thought Dad was still dreaming.' She explained that he had always been a bit of a dreamer, which was why he hadn't provided for her mother. She smiled. 'You won't believe the next bit,' she said.

'Try me,' I urged.

'Mum's friend told her that she had been so lonely she had often thought about asking Nell to live with her, but thought that I might be offended.'

'So your Dad wasn't dreaming after all, was he?'

'He certainly wasn't, and he obviously knew it would work, because they are very happy together.' She hugged me, and said, 'I can never thank you enough. I love my mother but she was driving us mad.'

I told her that it was her father who had brought about the happy ending, not me.

'Betty, after we had received your message, things were a lot happier at home, which meant that we remained friends. That meant a lot to both of us.'

I do believe that if families get together and talk about these difficult situations, then solutions can be found. There are still many old people who are entitled to help, financially and otherwise, who are too proud to ask for it.

The young never think they are going to grow old, but it comes to us all in the end. There is so much that young and old can give to each other, and something as simple as becoming a pen friend, for example, won't take that much time out of your life.

I do not think that the general public are aware of the many diverse situations that mediums have to cope with. I can understand that because in the beginning I was completely unaware of the diverse situations which I would have to tackle. Perhaps it's just as well that I didn't. I might have refused to take on the challenge.

CHAPTER FOURTEEN

I WAS NOW IN MY NINTH YEAR AS A MEDIUM, and still experiencing a wide range of phenomena every day – although, much to my delight, the smell of ether had disappeared. The variety was endless, and the picture-shows that were projected onto my bedroom walls were a constant entertainment. One night I saw a group of uniformed men. I thought at first they were policemen but as they had their backs to me I could not be sure. No matter how long I thought about it, the reason for this particular scene eluded me.

Then one day, two plain clothes policemen visited me and asked if they could speak to me. As I was busy, I suggested that they return in the evening. I had no idea what they wanted, but it kept me guessing all day.

When they returned, one of them introduced himself as an inspector, and told me that they had found my name and address in the diary of one of my young patients. She had been brutally murdered. I was mortified, especially as I had told her that she must be careful on her last visit. He asked me if I would help by using my gifts of mediumship; I agreed to do this, and for thirty minutes, I was able to give him specific details about the murder and the perpetrator. He appeared to be delighted with the information, and handed me a parcel, suggesting that I might receive further details from the contact, as it contained the victim's clothes. From these I was able to give a clear picture of her last moments and these were to leave a lasting impression on my psyche.

That same evening I saw a police car stop outside the house, and it stayed there for about fifteen minutes.

The inspector called again the next day and told me that he had asked his men to keep an eye on me, as I could be in danger. That really cheered me up! He also asked whether I would mind visiting a police artist with him.

'You'll like him,' he said. 'And it will be interesting to see how successful you are working together.'

I told him I would be happy to do so, and he called for me the following day.

There was an immediate rapport between the artist and myself, and I fell in love with his work. I felt that it would be a privilege to work with him. To begin with, he asked me to sit on a chair facing the easel, on which he had pinned a blank piece of white paper, explaining that he sketched with a charcoal pencil. Within a few minutes we were working together. I closed my eyes and was able to easily conjure up the face of the murderer, which had haunted me from the first time I had seen him. When I finished with my description I opened my eyes and there, facing me, was his exact image. I could not believe it! The artist was a genius. It was obvious to everyone that there had been an incredible telepathy between us; there were so many tiny details that I had not thought important enough to pass on, and yet there they were in the picture.

Needless to say, the inspector was delighted, and on the way back home asked me if I would help in other murder cases. I agreed, because I had found the whole process fascinating, but would later regret this decision.

On one occasion I was given a parcel of clothes belonging to the victim, and as I handled it I clearly heard the sound of a gun being fired. I turned to the inspector and said, 'This man was shot through the right side of his neck.' He confirmed this. 'He was also shot through the side,' I continued, because I can see a bullet hole by the side of his kidney.'

He looked at me in amazement, and said, 'You're spot on. We didn't know it was there until his clothes were removed.'

'But it made a hole in his jumper,' I protested.

He smiled, and said, 'I know! But it was so small we didn't see it. We must bring you in on these cases much earlier.' He was obviously pulling my leg!

Again, I was astonished by the clarity of the pictures I was receiving. I saw the victim walking to the front door of his home, and then I heard a shout, the victim turned around, and it was at that moment that he was shot. I saw a man running down an alley and disappearing into a cobbled yard, very similar to those seen in old stableyards, and then saw huge wooden gates being slammed shut. What I did not get was an image of the man as he ran away, although from the back view I could see that he was wearing a raincoat and appeared to be quite stocky.

After a while, I found that the images of the victims were taking over my life, and because the vibrations were affecting my healing, I decided to stop working on murder cases. I'm sure my spirit team were in agreement, because when the terrorist squad turned up on my doorstep asking if I could help with the Harrods bombing, my mind went blank and I was no use to them whatsoever.

Two years later I moved to Sussex, and on the second day in my new home I saw a policeman walking up the garden path. My heart sank, and I thought, 'Oh no, not again.' When I opened the door, he asked me whether I had seen anyone hanging around as there had been several cases of arson. 'In fact,' he said, 'the barn across the field has just been set alight.' We looked out of the window, and saw a huge plume of smoke wafting across the Downs.

Without thinking, I said, 'I think you will find that it's a group of children, probably no more than eleven or twelve.' As soon as I spoke I could have kicked myself.

'That's an odd thing for you to say,' he said, looking at me with a puzzled expression on his face.

Rather than have him think that I was peculiar, I told him that I had worked with the police before. His expression gave nothing away, but I could feel from his vibes that he thought I was a bit odd. He probably wondered what he had done wrong in his life that he should have me suddenly arrive in his patch!

About three weeks later he knocked at my door again. 'I've come to tell you,' he said, 'that we caught the arsonists setting light to a garage. Their ages ranged from eleven to thirteen.' He smiled. 'Just thought you'd like to know.'

We worked on several cases together, but my heart was not in it, and I felt increasingly ill at ease. I was pleased when this work petered out. I did help out in a particularly brutal double murder, giving a policeman some vital evidence, but he did not mention my name during the enquiries, for which I was thankful. Two years later my evidence was found to be correct.

Although I would never go down that avenue again, I was grateful for the experience, and it later proved an enormous help when I found myself dealing with victims of physical and mental abuse.

One such case was Glenda, a very attractive woman in her thirties who had made an appointment with me for healing. Whilst I was healing her I saw funnels of energy emanating from her body, and when I placed my hands over them the heat was incredible. This told me that there was a considerable amount of inflammation there, and I questioned her about it.

'I can't tell you,' she said. 'It is a private matter.'

'But your body must be bruised all over.'

'It is. That is why I'm here,' she replied.

'Okay,' I said, 'I'll get on with the healing.' Then a voice a said, 'I'm Mary. I want to speak to Glenda,' and I passed the message on.

Glenda held her hands up in horror. 'Oh no!' she said. 'I can't cope with her.'

'Why not?' I asked.

With her head resting in her hands, she muttered, 'Because I took her husband away from her, that's why.'

I pressed her to listen to Mary. 'She doesn't sound angry to me. Perhaps she can help you.'

Glenda looked weary. 'Okay, I'll listen.'

'Well, I hope you will, because she is telling you to leave your husband before he kills you.' I paused to listen to Mary. 'She's also telling me that you did her a big favour when you took him away from her, as she had never had the courage to leave.'

'I did that all right,' she said cynically. 'What else does she say?'

'That your husband is a sick man, and that no matter how hard you try to help him you will be the one who suffers most.' At this point Mary's voice faded, but I still felt a strong link with her, and felt that she was extremely compassionate. I passed this feeling on to Glenda.

It was obvious from this conversation that Glenda had been physically abused by her husband, and she began to tell me about it. When she had finished I urged her to think about Mary's message and she promised to do so. Glenda came to me for a further three sessions.

I met her again four years later, with her new husband. She told me that she thanked Mary every day for her message, as it had probably saved her life. 'My ex-husband will never change,' she said. 'Abusing women is a way of life for him.'

Trying to help women who have been physically abused is not easy. There are a hundred and one reasons why they are unable to leave their tormentors. All I could do was pass on survival messages to them, give them clairvoyance and try to heal them. But even when the outward signs of the abuse are no longer visible, the mental scars remain, and it is this that leads to deteriorating health and terminal illnesses.

It was therefore encouraging to be told how strong they became after healing, and how they have felt that someone was watching over them. This enabled many of them to turn their lives around and put the past behind them. I was thrilled, for I knew just how much courage it had taken for them to take those first steps to freedom.

Although physical violence within families is far more common than people realize, mental cruelty is more widespread, and the perpetrators, in most cases, turn it into an art form.

Most people are subjected to mental cruelty at some time in their lives and while there are many who can put the experience behind them and go on to lead a happy life, there are thousands who, for one reason or another, have to live with it. And there are countless thousands of children who have to share the humiliation of one or both of their parents. This humiliation spreads like a virus, and a great number of children who grow up in these circumstances go on to use mental abuse as a tool later on in their lives.

Janie's story is typical of the mental abuse that some women have to suffer. She and her husband were deeply in love when they married. Then she had a child. Although she had put on weight, Janie still had a nice figure, but her husband tormented her about her weight, night and day. She tried to lose the extra pounds, but was so shocked by his treatment that she failed to do so. Things went from bad to worse as she comforted herself with junk foods. Soon she was two stone overweight and the marriage was in deep trouble. Then a member of her family took her in hand and, with a lot of love and persuasion, helped her regain her petite figure. Unfortunately, her husband had found that he enjoyed the power he had over her. No matter how attractive she looked he would criticize her until she cried, then he would walk around singing and whistling, revelling in the torment his wife was suffering at his hands. When she could stand it no longer she left, taking her child with her. Her husband begged her to return, but it was too late. She felt that she had suffered enough at his hands, and refused to see him again. What a waste of a young family!

Over the years I dealt with hundreds of similar cases, some of them quite sickening. I was able to help in most cases, but the greatest gift these people received was the survival evidence which gave them an assurance that they were not alone.

I will never understand man's inhumanity to man, or to any living creature. What I do know is that it will continue until everyone comes to understand Universal Law, and the understanding of the need for a spiritual life that co-exists with the physical .

I believe that there is a sickness in our society that needs attention. When I was growing up, people were accepted for what they were, not for how they looked. We accepted that everyone was different, in stature and nature, and we either liked them or we didn't. As a child, it was always comforting to be greeted by someone who was fat and jolly. Skinny people were usually regarded as being a bit miserable, and what would now be normal was then regarded as boring. Everyone had unique personalities, and did not try to mimic others in any way. Now there are so many clones that they are being accepted as the norm. I find that frightening.

If the love that exists between two people is real, then size and shape should not affect that love. There are so many factors to problems with weight, but I believe that one of the main causes is a deep unhappiness brought about by constant criticism.

To be able to keep our bodies at a constant healthy weight we have to love ourselves. To achieve this, we must continually tell ourselves we think we are great and we deserve to be healthy and fit. Wanting to exercise and maintain a healthy diet will follow. Loving ourselves enables us to ignore unpleasant remarks and plan a happy future.

I do not think that I am alone when I say that I don't see the physical body when I am speaking to someone. It is the personality that attracts every time, and it does not matter whether they are the most beautiful man or woman in the whole world, if people are boring I have to make my escape.

I am often asked by teenagers how to acquire a pleasing personality. I tell them that they must be genuinely enthusiastic about seeking knowledge, and about making every day of their lives special. They should also be aware that no matter how much they think they know, it is but a drop in the ocean, because no one will ever know it all – but seeking knowledge is so exciting, so stimulating, that the experience stays with you for the rest of your life. That can only be a good thing.

Being a good listener is also a great asset, and one that has enabled me to gain so much from my spirit friends.

I cannot repeat too often that Universal Law multiplies the good and bad deeds, and sends them back to us when we are at our lowest ebb – for the ultimate impact. No one escapes. I am sure that if this Law were to be taught in schools it would eventually bring some sanity into this sad world.

CHAPTER FIFTEEN

IN DEEP MEDITATION ONE DAY, I heard a voice say 'Come with me,' and immediately found myself walking through a maze of hedges. I was unable to identify them, as they were totally unlike anything I had ever seen before. Some were broadleafed, while others were reminiscent of the yew, with the branches forming a circle-like structure. I thought at first that the lanes were of grass, but as I trod them they had the texture and fragrance of camomile. I gave myself up to the total peace and serenity of the atmosphere but, as avenue after avenue came to a dead end, and it appeared that I was going nowhere, this feeling was replaced with a certain frustration. However, because I like a challenge, I kept walking, determined to find a way out. I was also intrigued. Although I knew I had a companion, and could feel the immense power emanating from him, I could not see him.

A bright light appeared above my head, and as it moved forward, I followed it, and found myself standing in a field. Flashing lights lit up the sky, occasionally striking the field, reminding me of an electric storm I had witnessed once in Spain. And yet I knew that this was different. Then I was surrounded by mist, and began to float high above the field, becoming a part of the firework display. In turn, my body revolved, became still again, and was then propelled forward. I was exhilarated by the freedom of flight and the lack of gravity, and could have stayed like that for ever, a small part of the revolving Universe.

But just as that idea flashed through my mind, I found myself standing on the top of a mountain, with seemingly endless valleys, rivers, forests and mountain ranges stretching away into the distance, and I knew that I had come home.

The man spoke to me again. 'You must write it all down,' he said, and I was shown a book. I looked at the cover, which was misty, as though a film had been drawn over it. Speaking again, my spirit companion said, 'When the time comes all will be revealed, but first you have to work. You must provide the text.'

Then I was back in my healing room. I had no recollection of the return journey, but I felt as though I had been away for years. When I looked at the clock it had only been fifteen minutes.

From that day, I dreamed of writing a book about my experiences, but I knew that if I wanted to capture the attention of non-psychics as well as psychics, it would have to be written in a very special way, so that everyone could understand it.

I also knew that there was no possibility of my writing a book just yet. There was just not enough time, especially as I had added work-shops to my agenda. For the moment it remained just a dream.

For various reasons, I decided to have a sitting with that very famous medium Doris Collins, and she told me that I would be giving up hands on healing, to heal through the written word.

I thought that this was the most ludicrous suggestion; I was still working over seventy hours a week, and there were many people who depended on me. And yet, in my heart, I knew that my appointment with her had been arranged by my spirit friends, so that I could receive confirmation of their message.

Instead of comforting me, this knowledge became a worry. I had established myself as a professional healer over the last nine years and I could not imagine how I could possibly give it up. It was the most important thing in my life. Also, I was now living alone after an amicable separation from my husband, and I needed to work.

The whole idea of my writing a book seemed a total mystery, and was to remain so for the next two years. In the meantime life had to go on; dreams were only taken out of the closet and looked at very occasionally. Like so many people before me, I found that I could not afford them.

However, the memory of that wonderful flight remained with me all the time. The incredible feeling of being able to conquer the world as I stood upon the mountain top, with its fabulous views, reminded me that that was how I should feel every day of my life. I have tried to remain true to this feeling ever since.

Meditation has always played an important role in my life, and, as you have read, it enabled me to develop in a natural way. I believe it is the only way to avoid stress, and to link in to the spiritual help that we so badly need in our materialistic world. Meditating is not difficult. The first steps are very similar to day-dreaming, and we can all do that with ease. The more you day-dream, the more you will find yourself going that bit further into the realms of the spirit, or essence, of the Universe. It is a wonderful feeling for, as your mind energy expands, the pressure is taken off the body, freeing it from the prison of tension and allowing it to pulsate and find its own natural vibrational level again.

In my book, *Betty Shine's Mind Workbook*, you will find relaxation exercises which will lead you into meditation. There is also a powerful exercise called 'The Magician's Castle' which, if you are true to the first thought that comes into your head, will give you your own clairvoyance. I firmly believe in 'doing it yourself,' so that you can become independent and control your own life instead of depending on others to do it for you. That way you will become strong, and you will also be able to avoid the ever increasing number of 'control freaks' who are around. This type of person is weak and has a need to control. Unfortunately, their decisions are tainted because they lack the courage to go forward. I am asked time and again if there is an easy way to identify such a person – and there is. If you are living with someone who will not allow you to do anything for yourself, and who insist that they wait on you hand and foot, even though you are able to look after yourself, do not let them. They are making you dependent on them so that they have the upper hand. In other words, total control. Do not misunderstand me, many of these people do not understand why they behave as they do, and many of them are kind, but making someone dependent damages their psyche and weakens their resolve. If you have a controlling nature, use it where it is most needed – helping others who cannot help themselves. That can only have positive results.

Meditation is also invaluable because it eventually brings you face to face with yourself. You may not necessarily like what you see, but you will certainly know who and what you are, and from there you can restructure yourself. This in itself is a fascinating journey and, once you have jumped the first few hurdles, it can be a joy. Try it!

CHAPTER SIXTEEN

I T IS INEVITABLE THAT, AT SOME TIME, we must all vacate the chrysalis that is our physical body, and allow the essence of our minds the freedom it so desires. I believe it is in this area that mediums are irreplaceable. They bridge the gap between one dimension and another with survival evidence, giving comfort not only to the bereaved but also to the departed, enabling those on both sides to live their lives to the full.

It also takes away the fear of death for those in the last years of their lives. I had not realized until I became a medium, just how frightened old people are at the thought of dying. Because they are old, society does not expect them to show fear, and so they suppress it – and this makes them ill. When they are encouraged to speak about their fears, the floodgates open. I have seen quite tough individuals break down and weep, when they talk about the inevitability of death.

For these people, survival evidence provides the solace and courage they need when it is time for them to make the transition from one dimension to another, as the following story shows.

Maisie was a fairly active lady in her mid-eighties. Her daughter Deborah asked me if I could help her mother. Although Maisie was physically active, she had become increasingly depressed and withdrawn over the past year, and no matter how hard her family tried to help, she refused to divulge the reason for her unhappiness. I suggested that Deborah ask her mother to accompany her the next time she herself came to me for healing. This way Maisie would not be suspicious.

Deborah duly arrived for her appointment, and introduced me

to her mother. Maisie looked very fit, and was still a very attractive woman, but her eyes were dull and she looked sad. We chatted for a while, and then I asked her to sit in one of the armchairs whilst I healed her daughter.

About ten minutes into the healing, I glanced across at Maisie, and as I did so, I heard a voice say, 'For God's sake tell her to cheer up.' I hesitated to repeat this, so I waited for more evidence. It came. 'This is her husband, Eric,' the entity said. 'I'm very annoyed, because I can't get near her to comfort her. She has shut me out.' I passed on the messages to Maisie whilst I carried on with the healing.

At first she just sat and stared at me, and then she said, 'How do you know about Eric? Did Deborah tell you?' So I explained that I was a medium. 'I don't hold with such people,' she said. 'It's too spooky.' She stood up. 'I'm going. There's no way I'm going to stay here.'

Deborah tried to persuade her mother to stay, 'Come on, Mum,' she said. 'At least stay until I've had my healing.'

I decided to intervene. 'Deborah, I think you should take your mother home.' Turning to Maisie, I said, 'I'm sorry you've been shocked, but I thought you knew I was a medium as well as a healer. Go home and think about what has happened. If you want to return another time, I will be pleased to see you.'

When they had left, I walked back into the healing room and saw a spiral of energy in the centre of the room. A voice said, 'She will be back.' I do not know who was speaking to me – it certainly was not Eric – but the message made me feel better.

A month later, Deborah asked for an appointment for herself and her mother. I must admit I was rather surprised, and wondered what would happen this time around.

When I opened the door to them, I could not believe I was looking at the same woman. Maisie looked ten years younger and, as she smiled, her eyes lit up.

'I'm sorry I was so rude to you last time I was here,' she said.

Smiling, I told her not to apologize. I had understood her feelings. 'It must have been quite a shock for you,' I said as I showed her into the healing room.

'Well, it was rather.' She paused, and then she said, 'I want to thank you from the bottom of my heart. You have saved me from a fate worse than death.'

'What do you mean?' I asked.

'Misery,' she replied. 'You see, I thought life ended here, but since you gave me Eric's message, I've come to realize that we do survive death.'

'What makes you so sure?' I asked. 'After all, you weren't given much evidence.'

'Oh yes I was,' she replied vehemently. 'You may not have realized it at the time, but I could see my husband's face building up over yours as you spoke, and you also took on his mannerisms. It was Eric all right. That is why I was so frightened. And the more I thought about it, the more incredible it seemed.' She smiled, 'Perhaps I could come along now and then for a sitting.' I told her that she would be more than welcome.

Deborah told me later that the message from her father had turned all their lives around, and the atmosphere at home was now so much happier.

Maisie came to see me regularly for the next four years, and in that time received some incredible survival evidence, not only from Eric, but from friends and relatives as well.

She was ninety-two years old when she died. Her daughter told me that she never stopped speaking about her first visit to me, and how the experience had enabled her to enjoy the rest of her life.

Another person who visited me for healing was Tom. He was in his seventy-fifth year and suffered from chronic arthritis. He would often remark that he'd rather be dead than suffer any more pain. I gave him healing for six weeks, and during that period the pain receded and he was able to lead a more active life. It was then that he spoke about his fear of death.

'Where do we go?' he asked.

I explained that when the physical body dies, the mind leaves, and spins into another dimension.

'If that is true, he said, 'then there must be billions of people flying around out there. I'm afraid I can't accept that.'

When I explained that mind energy can reduce to the size of pin-head, or expand *ad infinitum*, and that there are many Universes, a look of amazement passed over his face as he tried to take it in. 'Crikey,' he said, 'I've never thought of it like that.'

I also told him that there were worlds within worlds, and that people were being reincarnated every second.

He scratched his head. 'Now you've lost me.'

'Well, you see, it's all about progression, and what we wish to achieve in other lives.'

'Sounds like a bloody lot of hard work to me,' he said. 'I thought I'd done my bit here.'

When I had stopped laughing, I said, 'I must admit, it is difficult to take in all at once.' As soon as I'd finished my sentence, I heard a voice say, 'I want to speak to my brother Tom. My name is Edie.' Fortunately, Tom knew that I was a medium, so I was able to pass the message on to him.

He sat bolt upright, 'Do you know, I've been waiting for weeks for you to give me a message. Well I never, my sister Edie. I can't believe it.' He told me that Edie was only twenty when she died.

'She's telling me that Marge and Joe would like to speak to you too, so we'd better get on with it.'

What followed was quite incredible. At least twenty people were mentioned, and about ten of them gave me personal messages – which were extremely evidential – to pass on to Tom. I was thrilled for him.

When it was time for him to leave, he said, 'That was the only way you could have convinced me that there is life after death.' He was a very happy man, and the reunion with his family and friends gave him a new lease of life.

I firmly believe that mediumship and the afterlife should be spoken about more openly on the radio and television. There are thousands of elderly people who so fear dying that it takes away the joy of living. They are also afraid to mention the possibility of life after death for fear of being subjected to ridicule.

The mediums in this country are much sought after world-wide, and yet the media still ignore this very considerable talent. Whilst this state of affairs continues, the older members of our communities are living in fear of the unknown, and are not receiving any kind of help.

The waste of their talent also angers me. I have been fascinated by so many life histories and by the variety of jobs that these elderly people have had during their lives, by the stories of their apprenticeships and the pride in their craft. Because of modern technology, many of them lost their jobs long before retirement age. The irony of this is that when that technology fails, for whatever reason, it is these same men and women who are called upon to save the situation. Surely it would be more sensible to give these craftsmen a part-time job teaching youngsters the basics, for no matter how advanced technology may become, we do still have things like power cuts, and machines do regularly break down.

One example of this is the computer industry. Seeking help from a variety of establishments, I am constantly being told that the computers have gone down and the staff are unable to help until they are restored.

Time and time again I have watched the humiliation of a young salesperson when they have found that the battery of their calculator is dead and they are unable to do simple mental arithmetic.

I am sure my readers have a thousand and one examples of the mindless way that some of our industries are run, and how they could all be improved by having wiser and older men and women passing on their wisdom and craft to the younger generation. The waste of their knowledge is criminal, and the nation is the worse off because of it.

This does not and could not happen in mediumship, for we are entirely dependent on our spiritual teachers for the knowledge and fine-tuning of our talents.

I get very angry indeed when I am made aware of the terrible injustices in the world today, and the way people treat each other. Any kind of softness is so often taken for weakness, and those who were born to love and give are usually used and abused. I have seen so many people born with a loving nature, subjected to abuse because of that nature. They gradually become brutalized, and try to change their personality, to toughen themselves – and this is the key to why so many are suffering mental distress. Children – especially boys – who have a gentle nature, are ostracized and tormented by bullies who in turn have been brutalized by being subjected to violence in addition to the cruelty often depicted on many television channels. I have spoken to hundreds of these children, and in many cases have only been able to bring about a successful healing in many cases by asking their parents to screen their children's programmes.

It can be extremely difficult for the parents because over the years, the gentle family comedies – which we can all appreciate – have been replaced by a modern concept of comedy. It may be fashionable, but it is very often distasteful and cruel.

Young people look for role models, and if they happen to choose the wrong one, they may turn into offenders against society. This is sad. I have dealt with many of these youngsters and have found that there is still a child waiting to get out and enjoy the life that they are entitled to have.

I believe that the way to keep children healthy and happy is to keep them active. Children sit down for hours in school, and when they get home they either do their homework or watch television. If only they could be taken to a leisure centre or pool for just half-an-hour when they leave school, we would have a healthier community.

The majority of parents obviously want the best for their offspring, but there are many who simply do not think about their physical and mental health. The child is part of a family, and must live as the rest of the family lives. But every human being is unique, and needs nurturing – not necessarily in the same way as everyone else. If only a fraction of time could be given to each individual, for their particular needs, then young people would be made to feel 'special'. When they have that feeling, they are able to accomplish so much more in life.

I am a parent myself, and I think it is the most difficult job on earth. Our offspring are with us night and day for what seems to be an eternity, and even though there are times when we'd like to send them to the far corners of the earth, we can't stop loving them, and always want the very best for them. When they eventually leave home we miss them, and worry about how they are going to manage by themselves.

Not so long ago, all parents had to worry about was whether their children were going to get pregnant or smoke. Now, they have to worry about glue-sniffing, fast cars, Aids, and a variety of mind-blowing drugs as well. The thought that their child might be harmed is forever in the mind of a parent when their teenage children are out late. This is not because they are being over-dramatic; it is happening with ever increasing frequency. The list of dangers is endless.

When these dangers can seem too great to be coped with by an individual family, they may be able to do some small things to help, such as taking their children to Judo or karate classes. This would teach them self-defence, and possibly help teach them some spiritual values too. And it would help cut down their television viewing time!

I have included these remarks in this chapter because I have seen what can happen, and have been broken-hearted by the waste of such young and beautiful lives.

In many countries throughout the world there are still storytellers who move from village to village, entrancing the children with their stories. These people are natural philosophers, and teach the children how to be successful within their own society.

We all need to listen more, especially to those people who have something worthwhile to say. It is only when we have lived to more than half of our life-span that we acknowledge that we do not, and never will, know it all.

I remember giving survival evidence to a man in his fifties, whose mother came through and chided him as though he was still a child. We both saw the funny side of it, but were impressed by what she had to say.

'You were always headstrong,' she told him, 'and you haven't changed at all. I've been watching you.'

At this point her son interrupted, saying jokingly, 'I hope not.'

Mum continued. 'You never look before you leap, and you're doing it again. I've come to tell you to stop before it's too late.' There was a pause. 'You know what I'm talking about, and I don't hold with it.'

'Do you know what she's talking about?' her son asked me.

'Yes, you're thinking of leaving your young family.'

'My God!' he said, 'You're all in it!'

His mother then told him a few more home truths and left. The man turned to me and said, 'That woman could always read me like a book, and yes, I am thinking of leaving home.' He went on to tell me of the problems he was having with his wife.

I urged him to give it more time. 'I think your mother may know something that you don't. You are obviously headstrong. Perhaps you should listen to her advice.'

We talked for some time, then he left.

I saw him again later that year, and he told me that he had been able to patch up the differences he'd been having with his wife. The family had stayed together.

'My mother always was a wise old bird,' he said.

When I was young, we were taught to respect our elders. It seems that there is very little respect these days, and yet it is the young who are missing out, for they could learn so much from the older generation. Let's face it, who do they run to when they are in trouble? It is usually their parents, but when they've been sorted out, they are off again, paying no heed to the good advice they have been given. This is the lack of respect about which I am writing.

Like so many people in this life, they have not learned that very valuable lesson, and one which could save them from many moments of anguish. The ability to listen.

CHAPTER SEVENTEEN

M Y DAUGHTER JANET WAS VERY CONCERNED about my living alone since the separation with her father, and she presented me with a beautiful tortoiseshell cat. I named her Sally.

I had lost my previous cat, Sadie, when I left Spain, and this had broken my heart. I was not particularly keen to acquire another, but when I saw Sally it was love at first sight. She was so beautiful. Alas, her beauty belied her nature, and from the moment this tiny kitten entered my home all hell was let loose. As one patient put it, as Sally flew from one armchair to another in the waiting room, 'that thing is a cat from hell'. Well! He obviously did not like cats, but she was a menace.

Nothing escaped her teeth and claws, not even my hands. She found my new carpets irresistible, and she tore at them. My furniture was given the same treatment. She walked precariously in between my ornaments, and I watched in horror as she defied me to remove her, staring at me with a look that said, 'Touch me and I'll break the lot.'

I longed for the day when the necessary vaccinations had been given and I could let her out into the garden. But when that day finally arrived, she proceeded to attack all the birds. Fortunately, I was able to throw the birdseed out of my bedroom window to a ledge she could not reach – though not for want of trying. I found her one day, hanging upside down on the windowsill, daring the birds to take the food. However, she had enough sense not to let go, as she would surely have been maimed if she had dropped from that height.

Why am I writing about my cat in a book on mediumship? I will tell you. On looking into the hall one day from my bedroom, I saw Sally, back arched, leaping around a specific spot. I walked into the hall and

165

saw a spirit entity. It was a man, holding a stick of some kind. As it was transparent and not a full materialization it was very difficult for me to take in any detail, and it disappeared before I received any message. But it was obvious from Sally's actions that she could see it too.

Every other animal I had known had always backed off from any kind of unusual energy. But not Sally! She had been poised for attack, and had been quite prepared to take on the intruder. I found it quite laughable, and it was this 'have a go' streak in her that eventually won me over. She confronted spirit entities on a day-to-day basis.

Sometimes she would prepare for attack in a crouching position, or leap into the air trying to touch the spirit, and there were times when she stayed in the air so long I thought she had levitated. There were also occasions when she would freeze, and stare into space, looking at something I was unable to see. I often wondered what it was that she found so worthy of her time, and then one day I was given the answer.

I had been sitting on the stairs in the large hall, observing one of Sally's staring periods, when, as quick as lightning, a black cat ran past me and down the long corridor that led to the bathroom. Thinking that it was a live cat, I ran after it, knowing it could not get away as the bathroom door was always kept closed, and it would be trapped. But when I reached the end of the corridor there was nothing there. It had disappeared. I walked back into the hall and Sally leapt toward me, playing in her most seductive, kittenish manner. She was, for the moment, quite normal. As I stroked her, I realized that the reason she was never afraid of spirits was that she had her own spirit world, and the staring episodes were an obvious fascination with the spirit world of cats. Maybe some of her past friends were visiting her. Who knows? She certainly held court often enough.

I felt that Sally had been sent to protect me, and this was confirmed one day when I was carrying out an exorcism. I never enjoyed this experience, but, from the time my patient appeared, Sally flew around the hall, hissing and clawing the air. She was obviously distressed. As soon as the exorcism had been completed, she was calm again, a good indication that her protective instinct was intact.

On another occasion, I had just shown a lady into my waiting when Sally walked in. As soon as she saw the woman, she jumped onto the top of one of the armchairs and proceeded to leap from chair to chair and along the back of the couch where my patient was sitting. The lady assured me that she was not frightened, but I still removed Sally from the room. I did not trust her. It was only when I began healing that I realized that the woman was suffering from severe mental stress, and the unusual energies that surround people in that state had disturbed Sally so much that she had tried to frighten my patient away.

I had seen the same behaviour pattern with Smokey, a small bitch I had once owned. A friend of my husband had decided to pay us a visit. Unbeknown to me, his wife suffered from deep depression and had been in and out of mental hospitals for some time. When the introductions had been made, I prepared some snacks and we all sat at the kitchen table. We had been talking for about thirty minutes when Smokey ran in from the garden and jumped on my lap. Smokey's hair stood on end as she came face to face with my lady visitor across the table, she bared her teeth, and tried to attack her. Fortunately, with the table between us, I managed to grab her and locked her away in another room until they left, but we were all shaken by this totally unexpected event. It was quite obvious that the dog had linked into the disturbed nature of my visitor, and had been affected by it.

Smokey was the first bitch I had ever owned, and I loved her dearly. Although ninety-nine per cent of the time she was a loving family dog, she did have one particular hate. As a young puppy she had managed to jump over the gate in the front garden, and had dashed around with glee on the pavement, enjoying her moments of freedom. Unfortunately an old man was passing at the time and, irritated with the animal's behaviour, he hit out at her with a stick. When I picked her up she was in considerable pain and was whimpering. I took her to the vet, who told me that she was quite bruised, but would be all right, and after a week's pampering she was her old self again. Or was she? She may have recovered physically, but not mentally for, whenever she saw an old man with a stick, she would fly at him. When we took her for walks we would scan the horizon, and if we saw an old man carrying a stick, we put her on the lead. The extraordinary thing was that she did not attack young men with sticks, so how could she differentiate, especially at long distances? It remained a mystery until I discovered and studied 'mind energy' decades later, and realized that the mind energy, especially in animals, is always way ahead of the physical. Smokey was able to detect her enemy before he had even come into sight.

Smokey scaled the fence one day, while she was on heat and, following this escapade, I was faced with a lovely golden retriever lying on the doormat in the porch every time I opened the door. Smokey was pregnant now, and I had to assume that this was the father. I was advised by friends not to feed him as this would discourage him from returning home. It did not work however, and so after two days I gave in and offered him food. He refused it, much to my amazement, and only condescended to drink a little water from the bowl I had placed before him. When he was still there after three days I became extremely anxious, and decided to call the police. They told me that they would take him to the dog pound. I was adamant that they should not have him put down if he was not claimed; I would find a home for him myself. Fortunately, his owner claimed him and the police kindly gave him my address. He called to see me and, after I had told him the story, he agreed that his dog should be controlled for its own safety. After all, he had crossed many main roads to get to my house, and could easily have been killed. The owner explained that the dog had crawled through a hole in the garden fence. All was well until Smokey had her litter; on that same morning I opened the door to find the same dog lying in the porch, with the largest bone I have ever seen. The frantic owner called an hour later, and told me that his dog had been in a terrible state, pacing back and forth all night; exasperated, he had let him out into the garden at four o'clock in the morning. When he called him thirty minutes later, the dog had gone, having gnawed his way through the fence.

I have studied energies for so long that I can now make sense of many things that had happened in my life. To those people who repeatedly tell us that there is no such thing as a mind that is separate from the brain, and outside of the body, all I can say, is let them explain away these stories. That dog lived three miles from my home; he knew the day, and the time that Smokey was giving birth, and was there for her as soon as she had produced the litter. He would have made a devoted father and I would have loved to have given him a home, but he already had loving owners, and they would never have parted with him. Something that has always puzzled me. Where did he get such a huge bone at that time in the morning?

All kinds of animals have passed through my healing room: mice, hamsters, birds, lizards, dogs, cats, and many more. Many of them were brought by children who had acquired the animals but had no idea how to look after them. I found myself educating not only the children but also their parents, and many pets survived who would otherwise have gone to an early grave.

Many dogs who had been given a life sentence by a vet were cured by healing. I believe that every doctor and vet should have a list of healers they could recommend to their clientele, if only to ease their own suffering when their pet has passed away. People need to grieve, and they need counselling, and healers fit this bill. Why then are their services not available? It is a grave mistake to leave people to go home and grieve alone. In many cases, their pet was the only friend they had. They need to know that the animals survive, albeit in another dimension, and that they can still talk to them. We should not ignore this issue.

I have been able, through mediumship, to help new owners of animals that have been rescued, by giving them a detailed description of the animal's past history, enabling them to understand the psyche of their new pet and prevent them from making any mistakes. I remember one dog in particular, called Mack. I linked to his past and, among other things, found that he had frequently had his meal taken away by a child in his previous family. When he had eventually bitten the child, out of frustration, the family had given him away. The child should

BETTY SHINE

have been severely reprimanded, but wasn't and this situation left the dog with a difficult mental attitude regarding its food. I picked up other small things that would help the new owners gain an insight into the working of the mind of their new pet. Later, they told me that they had carried out all of my instructions, and had eradicated many of the small idiosyncrasies I had identified – but there was still no way that the dog would let anyone touch its food.

Whenever I was asked to give an animal absent healing, I would first of all link in with it. This enabled me to diagnose the real problem and give the appropriate healing. Imagine my surprise when I found that I could reach them telepathically and 'listen' to their problems. It really was no different to a telepathic link with a human being, as their grievances and their love were made known to me in the same way. The owners found this hilarious, but when the laughter had subsided, admitted that the description of their animal's psyche was extremely accurate. One lady was so taken aback, she said, 'Fancy the little bugger telling you that. He knew it was supposed to be a secret!'

One dog, who was suffering from crippling arthritis, told me that he was ill because its owner had never taken it for a walk. When the lady called to give me the latest health report, I explained what had happened. However, although she was full of remorse, and told me that as a business woman she had never been able to find the time to walk the dog, she still insisted that it would be very difficult for her. She told me that she had quite a good sized garden, and thought that would suffice. When I asked her, in the nicest possible way, how she would feel if she were not to see the outside of her home for three years (which was the age of the dog), she realized how cruel she had been, and was full of remorse. 'I've been using him for protection, and haven't given a thought to his health,' she said. I suggested that she should hire a dog walker, which, to give her credit, she did. It took three months of healing and gentle exercise to cure the animal of its arthritis. Within six months he was running around, fit and healthy.

There are things that I am *not* told when I am asked to heal animals and, for that matter, people. With my diagnostic ability I have wondered why the healing was not working. Healers have been subjected to an enormous amount of ill feeling when healing has not worked, and because there are so many factors involved, it is necessary for anyone who owns an animal to assess the environment in which they are living. If this does not pass the necessary requirement, then something must be done about it. There is always an answer.

If an animal owner is old or ill, they should contact the local animal welfare groups and ask if someone can be found who would be willing to walk their dog, or find a friendly neighbour to do this. I know many people would love to help, but you must ask.

Throughout my teens, I had only one dream, and that was to become a vet. It was never to be. But it seemed that I was destined to heal animals, and so I became a spiritual vet.

Whenever we hear of dangerous dogs, I believe that it is human beings who have made them so. That is not to say that they deliberately set out to do so. It is a mixture of ignorance and stupidity, and sometimes, unbelievably, too much over-indulgence. We still have a long way to go in educating the public on the care of animals, but I think we are getting there.

In the end, we all have to right the wrongs we have committed, there is no escape. If this was more widely known, I think many people would think before they act.

Cruelty to any living thing is a moral and spiritual crime, and ways must be found to end the terrible suffering that so many living creatures have to endure. Because we have made them dependent upon us, it is our duty to care for and protect them. This is what thousands of people around the world are trying to do, and every single person can help in some small way.

CHAPTER EIGHTEEN

T HE PAST TEN YEARS HAD BEEN THE HAPPIEST of my life, and the presence of my spiritual mentors was a constant reminder of just how much I had changed in those years. I no longer questioned the whys and wherefores of the situation in which I found myself; I saw the results, and they were good enough for me. My spiritual medics could have done no more, because through me they had fought for the lives of so many, and won. Those who could not be cured were given peace and harmony, enabling them to make the transition to the spirit world in a dignified manner. My mediumship had evolved beyond all recognition, and the finest minds were able to communicate their thoughts and diagnoses. I knew at some time that the book I had been told I would write would have to be written, but not yet. There was another unexpected development, one that changed my life completely.

I had been living with a new partner for about four months when he told me that we would have to move from Sutton to Sussex. I was horrified at first, but soon realized that it was too far for him to commute for any length of time.

I knew nothing about Sussex. Apart from the years spent in Spain, I had always lived in Surrey, where the countryside and the hills had always been a favourite with my family. I thought of the wonderful walks we used to take through the beech woods, with the crackling leaves underfoot, and the smell of damp peat as the children and dogs trampled around in the undergrowth. Unfortunately, reminiscing did not help. It just reduced me to tears.

I was going to have to leave my lovely home, which was filled with so many memories – especially of the phenomena that still filled me with a childlike wonder, and which had made me realize there is so much more to life than the trivia which often surrounds our existence.

I felt guilty about having to leave my local clientele, who had all become friends. Although I had taught them self-healing, many were too set in their ways to be able to put this into practice, and inevitably needed to talk to me from time to time.

I thought of the hundreds of children I had seen, and the many animals that had received healing. They had all left a part of themselves in the ether of my home. The physical parting would be heartbreaking enough, but how could I leave behind the very soul of my present existence, namely, the spirit world?

I agonized for weeks, hoping that I might receive some guidance from my spirit friends, but nothing came. For the first time in all these years, I was alone. It was a desolate feeling. I had also suggested to my partner that we meet at weekends, but he would not agree. It was not one of my most brilliant ideas, but I was clutching at straws. I needed to make a decision, and it became obvious that I had to move to Sussex.

I contacted all my clients and told them of my decision. It was the most difficult task I have ever performed, because it made so many people miserable. They all insisted that they would try and make the journey to my new home, but I knew that for the majority, this would be impossible. Most of them booked a last appointment just to say goodbye, and as they left the tears flowed. The emotion of those moments left us all speechless. I cried more during those weeks than I have ever done in my life. I never wish to go through such an experience again.

When the time finally came for me to leave, I walked around the rooms, placing my hands upon the walls where I had seen so many faces. I walked to and fro in the large hall, where the funnel of energy had appeared. I sat on the couch in my healing room and remembered all the magical moments I had shared with so many thousands of people. I remembered the survival evidence which had produced so many tears of happiness and hope, and which had given the terminally ill the courage to make the most of the rest of their lives – in the knowledge that they were going to survive in another dimension.

When I left my home, I was too distressed to look back. I wondered whether my spirit friends would make themselves known to me again in the new house, but at the time I doubted it.

If it had not been for my newly acquired bitch Tessa, and my cat Sally, I think I could have quite willingly drowned in my grief.

When we arrived at the small cottage at the foot of the South Downs, with its far-reaching views and large garden, I tried to imagine our lives in this environment, and conjured up all kinds of wonderful images of days lounging about in the sun, watching Tessa revel in the freedom of her new surroundings. So much for the dreams! It was October when we moved in, and on the day we arrived the weather changed for the worse. Not a good sign. Because it had been necessary to make a quick move, there had been no time to arrange for a cooker, telephone, coal – as there was no central heating – and, too late, we discovered that the front and back doors were so flimsy that they barely stopped the wind that was howling around the house. Sitting in front of the window, with a blanket around my shoulders, it became obvious that without secondary glazing, I would probably die.

My friends would have been horrified had they been able to see me, knowing as they did my love of a warm and comfortable home. No wonder my spirit friends had been silent. They probably thought I was out of my tiny mind and no longer worthy of their attention. And I would have agreed with them!

Worse was to come. When we tried to fit both sets of belongings into the rooms, it became obvious that even if we could have reduced the furniture to a third of its size, it was not going to fit. In all fairness, I have to say that my partner had very little, and even though I had given away the largest pieces of furniture, I had still brought too much with me. We spent the first night miserable, cold and hungry. My cat didn't like it there either. Okay, I know I had been spoiled, but this was ridiculous!

Eventually, over a period of six months, we modernized our new home, but not before I was carted off to the local hospital where it was found that I was suffering from patches on both lungs because of a viral infection. I knew then that the cottage would not be a part of my future life.

The worst part of all this was the feeling that I had lost touch with my spirit friends. I was now embroiled, through my partner, in a materialistic world, and every day it seemed to be taking away more and more of my soul. Losing touch with the spirit world made me realize what a comfort they had all been and, the more I thought about the move, the more I realized that I had made a terrible mistake. Why had they not warned me? It could have been that with so many personal problems I simply had not been listening.

So I sold my home in Sutton, and this meant that we were able to move to a larger house nestling at the foot of the Downs. As it was only half a mile from the cottage, it did not take us long to move, and as it was now April, and the sun was shining, my hopes of a happy future were raised.

Within a few months Tessa and Sally had a new friend, a Yorkshire terrier named Flossie.

I made friends with one of our neighbours. Everything seemed to be going well, until she found out that I was a medium. We never spoke again. I felt as though I had been transported back to the middle ages.

I was able to put one room aside for healing, and started to work again. I was delighted when my spirit friends returned in force. I had missed them.

Our lives were such that it was necessary to entertain visitors from abroad, and it was on these occasions that my mediumship came to the fore. It seemed that everybody had family and friends who wanted to communicate. I did not mind passing on the messages, but did they have to come through during dinner? Having delivered the survival evidence, I found that my food had gone cold and I was left hungry. Not good timing at all. But, on the positive side, I had made some people very happy. In particular, I remember one Greek agent. A family member made it known to me that he wanted to communicate. I asked the agent if he would be interested, and he said he would be delighted, as he had never had any experience with mediums before. He confirmed all the messages that I gave him. Then he was told that he was going to lose his right-hand man within two months, and the real reason for the visit from his spirit friend was so that he could make suitable arrangements so that his business would not suffer. He could not believe this. He told me that the person in question had been working for him for twenty or more years, and that he was totally loyal. Before he left I asked him to think seriously about the message.

Six weeks later he called to tell me that the man had just given notice, and that he was going to leave in two weeks. Exactly two months to the day. Because he had not believed the message, he had not prepared himself; inevitably, for a little while the business did suffer.

Because these sessions only filled a little of the gaping hole that had been left by the absence of my close friends and ex-patients, my thoughts turned more and more to the book I had wanted to write. I decided that I should delay no longer and spurred on by the mediumistic message telling me that I would be healing through the written word – I picked up a cheap notebook and began to write. First I had to choose a title. Thinking about the minds that attached themselves to me when giving survival evidence, I decided to call it *Mind to Mind*.

I remember that first day. I sat for hours, writing like a lunatic – mainly because I was returning, if only in spirit, to my home in Sutton. As I relived those happy years, I felt that I had been born again.

After that first day, I allotted so many hours a day to my writing. On the fifth day I heard a voice say, 'Your voice will be heard.' This gave me tremendous incentive, because I knew by that simple message that the book was going to be a success.

It was also the beginning of a new cycle of phenomena. My old friend Father Time reappeared and spoke about the danger of more diseases from outer space descending on this planet because of the earth's sheath. I must admit that I had no idea what he was talking about, but it became clear when the whole world was made aware of the holes that were appearing in the ozone layer.

Whilst I was writing *Mind to Mind* I was able to shut out the materialistic side of my life for a while, and this enabled me to return to my regular meditation periods. I had felt so desolate without them.

Our first spring and summer in the new house had been pleasant but, as autumn approached, and the winds howled along the foot of the Downs, my heart sank. Remembering my first nightmarish winter, I had a sense of foreboding, which was realized, only too soon. The house was at the end of a long run of the Downs, and as the wind raged from the Steyning Gap, along this particular range, it hit us at full pelt. We discovered that our windows were inadequate, and once again, we had to consider double glazing. To go through this hell twice in eighteen months was just appalling. When the workmen arrived, they took all the windows out at the same time, assuring us that they would be replaced by evening. Unfortunately, some of them were the wrong fit, so we were left with tarpaulins that crumpled under the onslaught of the gales. This, coupled with the fact that we were faced with a morass of cement outside the house, where the builders had started on the new hard standing for cars, left me in a state of total despair.

As the winter wore on, and the back door of the house was practically torn off its hinges every time it was opened, I made a decision. Come hell or high water, we were going to move.

So it was, that in snow three feet deep, I saw the seventy foot long bungalow nestling in its own grounds, the surrounding village protecting it from the fearsome gales. It was love at first sight. In a dreamlike state I wandered in and out of the rooms. The discovery of a complete one bedroom flat, at the far end of the bungalow, filled me with ecstasy. This was going to be my new healing sanctuary!

Apparently, the previous owner of the property had been a well-known artist, and although she was in her nineties and had lost her sight, she had insisted on living there with her housekeeper until her demise. This information helped me a great deal when the phenomenon of the buzzers began. I was alone one day when the monotonous tone of a buzzer came from the flat. On investigation, I found the contraption high up on the wall of the small hall. A few seconds later the noise stopped and all was peaceful again. I set about trying to find out how this buzzer was activated, and decided to start with the lounge as this was the room in which the artist had spent a great deal of her time during her last years. There, beside the fireplace, was a bell pull. Fascinated, I decided to leave everything intact; after all, I was not about to upset the lady, as it was obvious that she still felt that it was her domain.

While the cat roamed the protected garden, marking her territory, the dogs ran up and down the long corridor, revelling in the freedom of so much space. I understood how they felt.

It was not long before another strange thing happened. I was cleaning the lounge one day, and felt a cat brushing against my legs. Thinking that it was Sally, I bent down to stroke her only to find that, apart from myself, the room was empty. I looked for Sally, and found her asleep under a hedge in the garden. So we not only had a lady spirit, but also a cat. I asked my new neighbours whether the artist had had a cat, and was told that she had befriended a stray that had never left her side. When she died, a friend gave it a home, but it had pined away. I asked for a description of the cat, and was told that it had been an ordinary tabby.

As soon as my healing room was complete, I was invaded by groups of my patients from Sutton. On one particularly busy day, I had to ask a group of three women to sit in the waiting room for fifteen minutes. When it was their turn to have healing, one of them said, 'I didn't know you had two cats, Betty.'

'I haven't. Sally's my only cat,' I replied.

They looked at each other in astonishment. 'But we've just been making friends with a lovely tabby. It climbed onto our laps in turn demanding attention, and we've spent all this time stroking it.'

'Where did it go?' I asked.

'We don't know,' one lady replied, 'We were distracted when you entered the room, and now it's gone.'

As there was no way that a cat could have entered my waiting room, I told them the story of the tabby cat and its owner. They were both astonished and delighted.

'I've never seen a spirit of any kind,' one of them remarked.

The other two ladies were equally adamant that this had been their first experience of a spirit sighting.

They made a point of coming down to Sussex every month for their 'top up' and a chat, but they never saw the cat again. Instead of being disappointed, they told me that it made their encounter with the cat even more special than it had seemed at the time, and they never ceased to talk about it.

The tabby was not the only spirit cat roaming around. Six months later a black cat made an appearance. The first encounter was when it leaped across our bed one night; after that, it was often seen springing around the house. Even though I spent months trying to find out about its background, it seemed that no one had ever seen a black cat around the property. I could only assume that it might be the same one who had attached itself to Sally in Sutton, and who had decided to join us in Sussex. After all, when you are a spirit, time and space mean nothing at all.

CHAPTER NINETEEN

PATIENTS OLD AND NEW SAW MY new healing room transformed by an amazing kaleidoscope of colours. At other times
the room was suffused with one predominant colour, the favourite
being a beautiful sunflower yellow. People also attracted their own
colours, and these were determined by their ailment.

The room, once energized, supported the most amazing material-
izations, and several times I saw a spirit child slip into the room by
way of a coloured slide. Grieving parents were transformed as they
were given proof of survival by their late children.

As I felt my spirit world return to normal, I knew, without any
doubt, that the material world in which we live made no sense to me at
all without its spiritual counterpart. There are complex variations of
this force and, like the spokes in a wheel, they complete the whole.
I knew now that, once having seen all of these variations, I could not
conceive of a life without them, and I was delighted when the gift of
healing made these visions available to others.

I also knew that I had to bring my experiences alive for others, so
that they could share the wonder of this mostly unseen world, and
share the gift that I had been given.

I found out, to my cost, that a book does not get written without a
great deal of hard work and discipline. I have never had a problem
with hard work, because the alternative would be boredom and that
for me, would be a fate worse than death. But discipline was not one
of my virtues. Although my mediumship had brought its own discipline, I scarcely noticed it, because other people's needs were greater
than mine and I always had company. Writing, on the other hand, was
a solitary occupation. After writing for hours, I would feel as though I

had produced several thousand words, when, in fact it was only a few hundred. With a permanently aching back and arm, I began to think that mediumship and healing was a doddle compared to this, and constantly wondered why I was putting myself through this agony. But I knew the answer, and plodded on painfully.

Luckily, help was at hand. Because of the interminable interruptions I suffered by writing on the kitchen table, I decided to change my venue and shut myself in my healing room, using the couch as my desk. The room was peaceful, and had the right vibes, and as I looked at the first blank page I saw that it was alive with words, dancing across the paper like ripples over a lake. Although I was unable to read them, I received the message loud and clear; someone had been elected to guide me through this new and exacting experience. I picked up my pen and began to write, and the words flowed. I felt humble and elated alternately, as I realized that my book had the spirit seal of approval, and all was well.

Over a period of time another guide joined the team. I became aware of him one day when I was struggling to remember the day, month and year, of a particular story. As I sat, face cupped in hands, staring at the page, the information appeared as if by magic. At first I thought I was dreaming, and then I burst out laughing. This was ridiculous! But, fortunately for me, it was for real. The facts remained on the page long enough for me to hurriedly write them down, and were confirmed later when I checked through my old diaries. From that time, whenever my memory failed me, I was given the information in this manner. Much later, when I had eventually learnt how to use a computer, the phenomenon continued, but this time the information I needed appeared on the screen, for all to see.

Although my days in Sutton now seemed so very far away, and my life had changed out of all recognition, I still felt that I had left a vital part of my soul behind. Then one day a friend called and told me that my old home had been pulled down, and was going to be replaced with a small block of flats. Although I was upset by this news, I knew in my heart that it was meant to be. It could never have retained its atmosphere, because the life had left, and I was warmed by the thought that the memories of the years I had worked there would remain for ever in the hearts and minds of myself, my friends and my patients. They could never be erased. They would be a more fitting memorial than the bricks and mortar; the spirits still lived, with me, and would continue to do so wherever I chose to be.

After months of hard work, the book was finished. It might not have been a literary work of art, but at that time it was the best I could do. A friend gave me the name of his literary agent, and I sent the book to him. He sent it back. He had turned it down. This did not make any sense. The spirits had not only told me to write the book but had also taken an active part in the process. So what was going on? I was advised to send it direct to a publisher, which I did and, eight weeks later, it was accepted. *Mind to Mind* was on its way.

When the book was eventually published, it immediately went on the *Sunday Times* bestseller list, and it was then that I knew it had all been part of a spiritual plan. I was kept busy for some time with the usual promotion tour, and received a massive amount of post, most of the letters sent by people needing help.

One of these was a friend of Michael Bentine. When I started writing this book I asked him if he would give permission for his story to be included. He agreed, and very generously offered to write it himself. This is his account of what happened.

'Once negative and evil forces lock on to one, help may be needed to shake them off – as my wife and I found some years ago. It was only after Betty had put in a lot of very hard work on my behalf that it became clear they had been banished for good.

'Many years before, as an inexperienced, single young man, I had become involved with a girl whom I later came to realize as having an hysteric and unstable personality. She was very manip- ulative, and eventually manoeuvred me into marrying her. Leaving out all the details of the disastrous relationship that followed, the deterioration in her mental health, over the years, was such that she eventually took her own life.

'The years I had spent with her had deeply damaged me, and

I felt an enormous sense of relief after her death.

'Two years later, I remarried. This time it was true love and things seemed set for a rosy future for my wife and I. But we soon sensed that there was a problem. It seemed as though my first wife had never truly departed, because my new wife was experiencing hysterical screams, through her psyche, which threatened the love that had grown between us. Also, we were continually meeting circumstances where things went wrong for us. Although I didn't recognize it at the time, I often reacted badly to these situations, and my ability to show the love that I felt was somehow blocked, leaving us both isolated.

'By this time we had moved, but the feelings followed and, in despair, I approached our Bishop. He told me to contact a Benedictine monk, whom we learned was one of this country's leading authorities on exorcism. This was Dom Robert Petitpeurre who, before he entered the Order, had been a theoretical chemist. We came to know him as a truly remarkable man, to whom such matters as coping with evil forces were a perfectly normal, if highly undesirable, part of life. He kindly came to our new house and cleared it of the unwanted influences. We visited him regularly at his Abbey until he eventually died.

'By then we had moved again and, in our new home, found that the earlier evil influences were trying to creep back. Dom Robert had previously told us there were three entities "sitting on my shoulder" – representing my first wife, her mother, and another distant female relation from that family's remote past. In the time we knew him, he had given me valuable advice on how to ward off immediate psychic threats and send back the "nasties" from whence they came.

'Then, one day, we heard Betty Shine talking on the radio, having just published the first of her *Mind* books. We bought a copy and found that my old friend Michael Bentine had written the foreword. I called him and asked how I could contact Betty. He put us in touch with one another.

'Betty, uncannily, understood the situation and told me that she would work on it. A few days later she called me and told the remarkable story of how she had faced these three beings – which I had not mentioned to her – on their own ground, and had spent many hours trying to persuade them to depart and leave my wife and I alone. She also told us that it had proved one of the most difficult tasks of its type she had undertaken. Eventually, she had only managed to influence the three entities by convincing them that whatever evil they used on us would inevitably turn on themselves. After that, Betty said, they withdrew, whereupon she placed an army of protectors around us to prevent their return. We have never been troubled by them since.

'We keep in touch with Betty – and also feel that Dom Robert is still keeping an eye on things.

'I am an engineer by profession, but have learned to be aware that there is much more in the world around us than appears on the surface, and my wife and I much appreciate the skills of people such as Betty who can help bring out that inner awareness which is so beneficial to anyone prepared to seek it.'

Exorcism is not something that I enjoy. In fact, I would be very wary of anyone who said they did. However, evil influences do abound and someone has to deal with them. Sometimes that person may be a member of the church, but it is usually mediums who take on the task.

I use the same method with remote viewing as I do when the affected party is with me physically, and this has proved to be very effective. Sometimes, for the medium, it is less harrowing.

The hardback version of *Mind to Mind* was on the bestseller list where it stayed for many weeks; as a result I received thousands of letters – and my life changed once more. I had written the book to free people from dependency, because it had been painfully obvious when I was in Sutton that I could not possibly see the hundreds of people who asked for an appointment. In the end, I had had to turn down those whose ailments were not life-threatening. With the discovery of mind energy I had realized that I could teach others how to manage their lives as well as giving themselves self-healing through exercises and meditation. Now, surrounded by a huge pile of letters, I realized that the majority did not want to be totally independent; they wanted to experience all of the phenomena for themselves, preferably in the company of a medium. It was certainly an eye-opener, and it was not necessarily, their fault.

From birth, we are taught to be dependent on others. First it is our parents, then our teachers, along with the family doctor and various other people who flit in and out of family life. We find that dependency is cosy, as there is always someone to protect us from the cruel world outside. Mothers, as a rule, protect their young and guard them from their enemies, and that is the right and proper thing to do. But there comes a time when children should be encouraged to take responsibility for their own actions and health, and this could start from as young as two years of age, by showing them the rudiments of self-healing (there is a chapter in my second book *Mind Magic* that will show you how to start). If this is done, your children will reach their teens knowing that life is what we make it, and not something that is served up on a silver platter. They will be able to embrace the outside world, and to deal with the everchanging issues, with confidence.

What is the secret of success in a career, and as a human being? I believe it is the way we handle the obstacles in our lives. If we have been successful in overcoming a difficult situation once, we know that if the same thing should present itself again, albeit under a different guise, then, by changing the formula a little, we can succeed again. In other words, we 'feel' a success. However, if we fail that first time, then we live in constant dread of the same thing happening again. This, in turn, introduces negative influences that affect other parts of our lives. Throughout our lives we will be presented with obstacles of one sort or another, and we have to deal with them.

Reading through the mountain of letters taught me a great deal, for I realized that those asking for help were not failures. They had taken the first step in their healing programme by writing the letter, and the second step by asking for help. If we are not strong enough, or qualified enough, to take the first steps ourselves, then we must lean on others until we are strong enough to continue alone. Meditation is a fantastic way of dealing with adversity, for it introduces you to your higher self, from which we draw our inspiration and strength. If we can deal with eighty-per cent of our problems ourselves, then we are entitled to seek help when the other twenty per cent becomes too much for us to handle alone.

The letters also revealed just how much psychic phenomena prevails in our lives. It was almost as though my revelations had unleashed a tide of frustration, where ordinary people had been so frightened of other people's reactions that they had formed a wall of silence around themselves. Inside these walls, they remained a prisoner of their experience. I learned that in many cases this fear had also left a legacy of disease, and the knowledge that there was someone who would understand had enabled them to shed their fear as they wrote their very graphic accounts of their experiences. It was a happy experience for me when the realization dawned on me that perhaps my book had been the key that had opened so many prison doors, and that people would have the courage to face their antagonists, in the knowledge that they were not alone.

For the moment I had my own antagonists, the media. The requests for me to appear on television, radio and for personal interviews, were relentless. The presenters and journalists alike were intrigued by Betty Shine. Was she for real, or simply mad? They had to find out. And if she was not mad, then perhaps she could be made to appear so, which would make a good sensational story. Fortunately, my spirit friends never deserted me, and whenever I gave an interview for a paper, or for radio and television presenters, the phenomena, survival evidence, clairvoyance and healing, gave them something to think about. I was frequently, beseiged by bogus journalists, who tried to get 'something for nothing' by pretending they were freelancing for major daily newspapers. But on the whole I was treated very courteously by all concerned, and some of these journalists have since become good friends.

One of the radio presenters also became a close friend. His name is

Peter Quinn and, at the time, he was producing a programme called *The Eleventh Hour* on Southern Sound. There was a tremendous rapport between us from our very first meeting, and the first programme was so successful that Peter asked me if I would appear on alternate weeks. The phenomena we experienced during the following year was unbelievable, and I included one of the stories in *Mind Magic*.

It was during this period, after I had confided in Peter that the sheer volume of requests for help had left me feeling inadequate, that he suggested that I make self-help tapes, which he would produce. There was no suggestion of money changing hands because his offer came from the heart. By this time he had also met my daughter Janet, who was, at that time, a 'Wheel of Yoga' teacher. He persuaded her to make her radio debut on *The Eleventh Hour*, and this was such a success that she was able to take over when I left. Later, he persuaded her to make her 'Mantra' tapes. Peter has produced all of our tapes over the years, and they, in turn, have given others the strength and knowledge to either help themselves, or have complemented the absent healing they were receiving.

If I had been amazed by the number of letters I had received when the hardback was published, nothing prepared me for the onslaught when the paperback was distributed world-wide. I was now receiving letters from the farthest corners of the earth, and every one had to be answered. It was a daunting task and threatened to overwhelm, and finally bury me, beneath mountains of paper. I worried constantly that someone who had written might be dying alone, and had reached out to another human being for a sign that someone cared, and that my answer would be too late. Eventually, of course, common sense prevailed. I knew in my heart that I could not save the world, but as I had fought for the lives of my patients before, I knew that I would help as many people as was humanly possible. I discussed this with Janet, and she agreed to work with me every day to this end, but the task was so monumental that I had to take on another helper. Eventually, Janet gave up her teaching to work with me fulltime, and it is a credit to her that my absent healing service became so successful.

In between my appointments, I sat and read each individual letter.

Then I mentally placed the name, address and problem into the healing network. The letter was answered by my writing a reply on the envelope, which Janet would then copy onto a printed letter. This was the only way I could read every letter I received. It proved so successful that we have kept the same method, with slight variations, to the present day. Inevitably, there were those who believed that their letter had never been read, and that the lists of books and tapes they received were only a means of extracting money. Nothing could have been farther from the truth. If I had wanted to make money I would surely have found an easier way to do it, for I am not bereft of talent.

There was also the added problem of postage. A first letter is rarely accompanied by a stamped addressed envelope, so we were faced with the phenomenal cost of postage, especially as it entailed sending letters all over the world. Although a request for return postage was enclosed in my reply, it was only by having the request printed in the second book that some of this burden was lifted. But to this day I still receive letters without a stamped addressed envelope, and the cost of a reply is still my responsibility.

I hope that explaining these procedures will give an insight – to all those who have asked for help over the years – into the way myself and my team work. We do care, about everyone, and if we sometimes fail to make this clear, be assured that your requests will never be ignored. I think it would help if you could feel the love and understanding that abounds when we are dealing with your mail. Many times a letter has reduced us to tears, and left us all feeling like wet blankets for the rest of the day. It is only the knowledge that there is an incredible spirit team helping that enables us to keep going. With your help and understanding, I hope we will be able to do so for many years to come.

With the publication of *Mind to Mind* came a completely unexpected phenomenon. The events recorded in the letters were various, but were caused by one and the same thing, and that was my photograph on the cover of the book. People were being drawn to the book in the stores, and, whether or not they had had any prior interest in the paranormal, they bought the book. There were those who were healed just by looking at my photograph, and others who claimed that by holding the book they were able to put themselves into an hypnotic state whilst applying self-healing. Still more saw my face changing as they looked at the photograph, and gave me a detailed description of people who had been seen to overshadow me whilst I was healing. I remember one letter in particular, written by a man who had been unable to work for fourteen years because of a chronic back condition. He told me that he propped the book up on the kitchen windowsill whilst he washed the dishes because my picture made him feel peaceful except for one day, when something gave him a terrific blow in the middle of his spine. He screamed out in pain and crumpled onto the floor. Minutes passed before he made the effort to get to his feet, and when he did, he found that he had been completely healed. For the first time in years he was free of pain. He waited six weeks before writing to me, in case the pain returned. Two years later he was still free from pain, and was working again. This story was the forerunner of hundreds of similar situations and healings. There were people who had been bedridden and were able to walk again, after simply holding the book, and many who saw their late friends or relatives superimposing their features over my face. The stories were endless. Critics may say that they were all from gullible people; they would be wrong. The letters came from men and women from every walk of life, and of every nationality.

At first, I was rather stunned by this, and didn't quite know what to make of it. But, as soon as I had accepted that it was actually happening, I was faced with yet another phenomenon. Apparently, my readers were having their own psychic experiences whilst actually reading the book. These were as varied as the other stories. Some felt as though they were levitating, while others could feel tingling throughout their bodies, and a tremendous sense of wellbeing. Everyone mentioned the total peace that they felt as they held *Mind to Mind* in their hands, and the majority wrote that reading the book had been a spiritual experience they would never forget. The miracles brought about by my first book appeared to be infinite, and I wondered how it would end.

I am sure of one thing, and that is that it had all been brought about by spiritual intervention.

CHAPTER TWENTY

THROUGHOUT MY LIFE I HAD ALWAYS BEEN a very private person. This may have been because, as a child, I had felt unable to share my psychic experiences, and also because my dream world had always seemed to be more real than reality. However, I have always had good friends of long standing with whom I could share my life, and who I have been able to trust. Since moving from Sutton circumstances had prevented us from meeting often, but we were nonetheless always there for one another.

In the aftermath of the publication of *Mind to Mind*, it seemed that my life was being taken over by others and my friends were beginning to fade into the background. This caused me great concern, until eventually I spoke to them about the dilemma, and we all agreed that no matter what happened in our lives, we would never lose contact.

Now it seemed, that my privacy had been lost forever. I found that I was sharing my home with a team of helpers, patients, children, cats and dogs, and the spirits.

It was not what I had visualized at all – and it had all happened so quickly.

In the midst of all this activity, I was trying to write my second book, *Mind Magic*. The idea had evolved from all the different comments and requests I had received in the post over the past two years. It was to be a teaching book, one where readers could try the self-help routines for themselves.

Something else was worrying me at this time – my own health. I had been experiencing bouts of palpitations, breathlessness, tachycardia, and numerous other small but nonetheless unpleasant symptoms. Because of some emotional and financial problems, I thought these symptoms were due to stress, until one day, during a medical check, I was told that I had a heart murmur. As I had been given a clean bill of health only two years previously, I was unable to accept the diagnosis. However, when I visited my own doctor and asked him to give me a medical, he confirmed the diagnosis, and told me that I should see a specialist at once.

I still could not bring myself to believe that I had anything wrong with me. I asked myself why? Why had it happened to me? I had been a vitamin and mineral therapist for thirty-five years, had never smoked, only drank alcohol on special occasions – and very little even then, as I actually did not like it very much. What had happened to affect my heart in this way? Perhaps it was the butter and cream I had consumed in my younger days. No matter how many times the thoughts whirled around in my mind, I could not ignore the fact that something was wrong, especially as I had been putting on weight in a rather alarming manner over the past three years. I was no different from hundreds of other people in these circumstances; I had simply refused to face the fact that I was ill, because I was so busy.

I checked out several heart specialists in London and chose one who was highly recommended by his own profession. We met, and I was given a medical check and x-rayed. The specialist told me that I had been born with only two cusps to my aortic valve, instead of three. That cleared up the mystery of why, even though I had been an opera singer, I had always found hillwalking difficult. He also explained that, although the condition was life-threatening, I would probably be able to live quite well for some time. I can't remember how I got home that day, but I do remember thinking that it was 'sod's law'. I had looked after my body and mind all my life, and I had been born with a genetic defect!

Then I was given a medical book that had been borrowed from a hospital. On turning to the page explaining the cusps, I read that having only two cusps meant that they would calcify. This in turn could lead to a sudden death between the ages of forty-five and sixty. As I was fifty-nine years old at this point, you can imagine how I felt! I felt really chuffed! Naturally, my family was very shocked. For the first time in our history, no one had anything to say.

I decided not to burden others with my problems, as most of the people I knew, friends and patients alike, had enough of their own. Patients were waiting; letters had to be answered, absent healing had to be given, and I had a book to write. I was not brave, I was frightened – not of dying, but of the way in which I was going to die. But there was nothing I could do about it, and although I had healed so many people, and seen so many miracles, I knew that the problem I had could not be dealt with by spirits. Or could it?

During this period, whenever I gave survival evidence, I wondered how long it would be before I joined my friends in the spirit world. My family had often joked that they would never be rid of me, even after my death, because I would haunt them. Thinking about my situation, I felt that it might not be too long before they found out!

Thank God for my work. It kept me busy and left me with little time to brood. Also, the most extraordinary things were happening through healing and manifestations, and I was delighted when the spirit children turned up in force, an obvious show of support. The overwhelming happiness that these children gave to their parents by way of survival evidence was a total joy. Some of them had only died in the past year, and two teenage boys returned with positive evidence before they had even been buried.

My healing room had taken on a life of its own. It was a different colour every time I entered the room, and I could see misty figures floating around. Children could also see them, and one little boy I was treating described them in detail to his parents. Animals too paid me a visit. But in spite of all the activity, the atmosphere was serene, and it was in this room, at the end of the day, that I found the peace I needed to fill my soul and write my second book.

Remembering all the important issues that had been raised by the letters we received, I tried to give my readers the necessary back-up they required. Again, whilst working on my project, I was given invaluable help from my spirit friends, and the months and years that I had forgotten appeared on the paper for a split second. The knowledge that I had this kind of back-up gave me tremendous strength.

Out of this came the ability to link into a spiritual source, which provided the inspiration.

Writing a book is rather like being pregnant, with nine months of discipline and a rather solitary existence, followed by birth, and a feeling of total exhaustion.

Before the publication of *Mind Magic*, I hoped and prayed that I had written a book that would inspire others to seek a future, and give them the ability to heal themselves and their friends.

When *Mind Magic* was launched, everything had been arranged for television, radio and journalist interviews, along with public appearances. We were all ready to go, when one interview after another was cancelled. This was because of the Gulf War; there was no space for any other kind of publicity at that point, which was understandable and right. Families scanned the news on television and in the papers for information about their loved ones. I thought the book would be buried. Then I received a call from my publisher, *Mind Magic* had gone straight to number one on the bestseller list. I could not believe it, and, to be honest, I don't think my publisher could either. My spirit team had been 'at it' again.

I was thrilled when, throughout that long sad winter, I received hundreds of letters from families who had gained strength from reading my book. It seemed that it had been published at just the right time.

The following year saw the launch of the paperback version, which had only been around for six months when I began receiving letters from people telling me that, with the help of the book, they had been able to start healing groups of their own, which had turned out to be very successful. I was thrilled. This was exactly what I had wished would happen when I was writing it. I felt very strongly that the healing touch and words of love had, in many families, taken a back seat, causing many family units to break down. The local postmen delivered the mail in sacks, and there were times when I thought my helpers and I would disappear for ever under the mounds of paper.

This should have been a very happy time, but my health was deteriorating rapidly, and it was becoming more and more difficult to hide the fact.

I was, at this time, giving fortnightly workshops, which invariably went on for five hours. The only way I was able to carry on was by putting my own exercises into practice, which enabled me to give the impression that I was fighting fit. Alas, when I got home in the evening, I would collapse. I was very sad when I had eventually to put an end to these meetings, as requests for tickets came in every day, and I felt I was letting people down. I know many of my readers could not understand why it wasn't possible for me to continue, and that is why I am putting the record straight here. I was not about to make anyone feel negative, after having produced two positive books, and, by public request, I was about to write another.

The title of my third book was *Mind Waves*. It had proved an impossible task to answer all the questions that were put to me, so I structured this book in a way that I hoped would shed light on the whole of the paranormal. My discovery and study of mind energy had convinced me that the mind controlled the whole, and it was during the writing of this book that I was given the incredible phenomena that put the seal on that conviction. The following stories are extracts from *Mind Waves*.

In June 1990 I decided to take two weeks holiday in Spain. The first night in the rented villa I was feeling very ill. Because I was worried that I would not be able to finish *Mind Waves*, I looked up at the ceiling and said, to any unseen spirit that might be lurking around, 'If you want me to carry on with this work, do something.'

When I woke in the morning I accidentally touched my body on the left side just below the heart. It was extremely painful. When I investigated the source of the pain, I found a red scar the length of my forefinger, with seventeen stitch marks. And around the scars were seventeen clamp marks. I recognized them instantly, from previous operations that I had undergone. For a moment, all I could do was stare in disbelief.

Over the years my patients have reported the manifestation of scars after I had performed psychic operations on them – but not, to my knowledge, with stitch and clamp marks. As I had been alone all night, they could only have been made by a spirit surgeon. Obviously, I could not show the scar to everyone but my family and one or two friends saw it. My symptoms disappeared completely, but the scar was still faintly visible six months later.

It was a great relief to me as I was able to continue to heal over the next few months, as well as writing the book, and it was during this time that I was asked to visit some crop circles.

In 1991 I was invited to visit some crop circles – in Wiltshire, where most of them seem to occur. I took my tape recorder with me as, over the years, many strange noises had been taped whilst I was giving healing. I wondered whether there might be any unusual energies in the circles, and if so, whether they would be healing energies. I had no preconceived ideas about the nature of these circles; I had a completely open mind.

I had travelled with friends, and when we were nearing our destination, we saw a most beautiful crop circle formation which had appeared the previous night. It was in an inaccessible position, but as it was carved out of the wheat on the slope of a steep hill, it could easily be seen from the road. To our surprise, other new circles had also appeared in the same vicinity.

The first two circles we entered were extremely interesting, one small new one having been formed overnight beside an old one. It was almost as though it had given birth! However, because the circle was so new there were a lot of other visitors about, so we didn't stay long.

We then made our way to some circles which had been formed the previous week. Leaving the car, we waded through the wheat and eventually sat down in one of the circles. I put the tape recorder down beside me and switched it on. My friends did the same with their recorders. I closed my eyes and relaxed.

I had a feeling of absolute peace and harmony, and had a

vision of lights, almost like searchlights, being beamed down on to the ground. I do not know whether these lights had anything to do with the formation of the circle. Ten minutes later, I rewound the tape and played it back. The noise it produced was unbelievable, rather like the hammering of a road drill. My friends had nothing at all on their recorders, and thought mine must be faulty. One of them asked if she could record on my machine, and I agreed, but suggested that as I was a medium it should be placed by my side. This she did. When she played it back five minutes later, it produced the same noise, which we had by now nicknamed the woodpecker – admittedly rather a loud noisy one. It was then suggested that the three tape recorders should be placed in a pile to see if the sound could be transferred. This time none of the recorders had any sound on them.

The tape recorder I had used was practically new, so I was almost certain that there was nothing wrong with it. But I was prepared to keep an open mind on the subject.

For years I have recorded my healing sessions, as the energy produces a sound like rushing water and this fascinated my patients. A week after visiting the crop circles, I put a new tape into my recorder during a healing session. When I played it back, there was the woodpecker hammering away. Thinking now that the machine was indeed faulty, I decided to record without actually carrying out any contact healing. I played the tape back a few minutes later and the woodpecker had gone, leaving only the normal energy sound. I suggested to my patient that I did a further five minutes contact healing, which I recorded. The woodpecker returned.

I decided to speak into the recorder, simply saying, 'I am not healing now,' because I felt there was an intelligence involved. On replay, the woodpecker had gone. Then I spoke into the recorder and said, 'I am now healing.' It returned. My patient and I were so fascinated that we continued in this fashion for over two hours. At one time I tried to trick it by saying that I was healing, when I wasn't. But there was no response from the woodpecker proving that there really was an intelligence behind it.

This phenomenon stayed with me for three years.

I cannot possibly list all the strange phenomena that I experienced during that year, but the next story will prove that the sound did not come from this dimension.

I was giving healing to one of my patients, and her friend was sitting in the garden, just outside the healing room. It was a lovely day, and I decided to leave the french windows open so that we could enjoy the cool breeze.

I switched on the tape recorder. All was peaceful. Suddenly, there was an incredibly loud noise outside. Looking out of the window, I saw a police helicopter circling the area at roof top height. The friend who was in the garden ran into the healing room, frightened to death. The helicopter continued to circle for a long time; we couldn't talk – our words were drowned out by the noise.

Later, when I had finished healing, I rewound the recorder and played it back. The sound of the woodpecker had completely drowned out the noise of the helicopter. I will let you draw your own conclusions.

A slightly different type of phenomenon happened the day I took a new tape from its plastic wrapper and put it in the recorder ready for my next healing appointment. When I played it back I found myself listening to a conversation that I had had with a journalist three months previously. The only recorder in the room at the time had belonged to the interviewer.

Having decided to buy a computer, I spent quite a lot of time tearing my hair out, and sometimes losing a whole day's work because I hadn't the ability to find what I needed in the maze of 'Help' menus. They didn't help me at all. Eventually, I managed to understand the basics, which made the task of writing a whole lot easier. But the spirits were at it again, and information that I had forgotten appeared on the screen, along with other personal messages about my life. It seemed that there was nothing they could not infiltrate.

I worked feverishly that year, determined to finish the book before I met my Maker, because it was quite apparent to myself and everyone close to me that I was very ill indeed.

When I had written the last words, and the manuscript had been posted to my agent and publisher, I allowed myself the luxury of thinking about myself, determined to face the future with positivity, no matter what the outcome.

The delivery of the book also coincided with the end of my second marriage.

CHAPTER TWENTY-ONE

I WAS ADMITTED TO HOSPITAL IN JANUARY 1992. The tests that were carried out showed that, without open heart surgery to replace my calcified aortic valve, I would die. I was told to go home and think about it before making a decision. There really wasn't much to think about! My quality of life was so bad, I felt I had nothing to lose. The plus side was that my heart was healthy enough to have the operation.

Not only did I have to come to terms with my possible demise, but circumstances were such that I was going to lose my home at the same time.

Throughout my life I have always tried to make a negative situation work for me, and I decided that this would be a good time to try out all the exercises and advice I had given to my patients in the past. It is always easy to hand out advice when you yourself are healthy, but I began to wonder if it would work for me when I was so desperately ill.

In the past I had helped patients who were about to have operations by teaching them how to communicate with their own bodies, to cut out most of the shock factor. I decided to work with my own mind and body in this way. First of all, I interrogated doctor and surgeon friends, and forced them to tell me the truth about the open heart procedure. When I had the whole picture, I mentally carried out the process, step by step, every night. I was determined that there was no way my body was going to have a nasty surprise. As time passed I was given, mediumistically, extra bits of information about the operation.

I also energized my body through exercises and meditation so that it would have the best possible chance of recovery. It may sound gruesome, but the method gave me such peace of mind that I found I could not wait to get to bed every night. At the same time, I was not only

BETTY SHINE

facing the reality of the situation, but also realizing the benefits of my own exercises, which enabled me to leave my body to fend for itself whilst I floated off into another dimension.

In the past many of my patients had told me how grateful they had been for the tuition and the exercises; now I was experiencing it myself, under the most dire circumstances, and was delighted to find that it worked! I was also aware that my mother was with me at all times, and felt the enormous comfort of my spirit team. The energy that surrounded me was fantastic.

I was also pleased that I had found the strength to get rid of all the negativity that had surrounded me for so long. Through my own studies, I have seen the effect it has on the immune system, causing the most serious dis-ease in the mind and body; no matter how much healing is given, this continues until the root of the problem is removed.

My family and friends set up a healing circle, and Michael Bentine called to say that he had also formed a circle for me, so I felt very secure when I entered the hospital for the operation.

I arrived in the late afternoon, and was to be operated upon early the following morning. I had an extraordinary feeling of peace, so the healing certainly seemed to be working, and I had great faith in the surgeons – both in this world and on my spirit team. What more could I want?

There were one or two things that had happened during my own mental operations that I wanted to verify. One of the nurses told me that she would be a spectator at my operation, so I told her what I had seen clairvoyantly, and asked if she would let me know whether I had been correct. It was important to me, as my study of the mind is an ongoing factor.

I have often been asked if I was afraid, and I can honestly say that I wasn't. I was not being courageous, it was simply that through my career as a medium and healer I had lost the fear of death. I had also seen so much suffering in others, and had experienced it myself, that I knew I did not want to have a poor quality of life, if I could be bouncing around happily somewhere else.

There was one episode that amused me. My family had gone, and I was waiting outside the X-ray department for some final checks. There were several men and women waiting with me, but trying to converse with them was impossible because they were all Greek. One man in particular was in a terrible state, and I found myself holding his hands and comforting him. He could speak only a few words of English, and I thought how awful it must be to have to undergo this type of surgery, in a country other than your own. Later, I mused that he would probably get through it and I would die.

I woke up in intensive care, lined up with several other people, and I saw that we each had our own nurse sitting at the bottom of the bed. My first words were, 'Am I going to live?' So that worry had definitely been in my subconscious somewhere! My nurse smiled at me, and told me that I was doing better than everyone else. I'm sure all the patients were told the same thing, but it was nice to hear. I don't know what nationality she was, but she was warm and caring, and looked to me like an angel. I have always been sorry that I was not able to thank her for what she did for me. Those nurses are so dedicated, and I wonder if they are ever aware of the deep gratitude the patients feel at their first sight of them. Even though I was in a drugged state, I could see the man I had comforted. We had both survived.

Within a few days I was walking up and down the corridor of the hospital, and meeting other patients doing the same thing. My Greek friend seemed to be doing well, and he smiled every time we passed one another. It was not long before I found out that heart operations are quite commonplace these days. There is a certain comfort in numbers, and the fact that there were so many patients recovering at the same time as myself removed the feeling of isolation.

The young nurse who had been a spectator at my operation was able to confirm my clairvoyance.

I had been in the hospital for three days when, one morning, I woke to find the whole room filled with a deep blue haze – so deep that I could not see the door. The energy it gave out was amazing, and I felt so uplifted that I experienced the familiar feeling of levitation, even though my body was lying on the bed. The healing circles were obviously working hard for me, and I send my deepest thanks to all who played a part in my healing. Nine days after the operation I was ready to leave.

I was told that I must exercise as much as possible every day. It just so happened that my return home was also the beginning of a heat-wave – in May! But I did my best; at first walking round and round the garden like a demented fox, and then two weeks later venturing out over the fields at the back of the house. It was very hard work, but I was determined to follow all the instructions I had been given, as I had to prepare myself for the launch of *Mind Waves* the following January.

In between the exercise routines, I found that I could release myself from the pain by way of meditation, and could link in with my healing network to give masses of absent healing. Judging by the positive response we were receiving through the mail, it worked. It is amazing how much pain one can bypass with this system.

However, strange things were happening to me. Black mists were obliterating my sight, sometimes lasting for fifteen minutes. It was quite frightening. Also, instead of the pain decreasing, it was getting worse. None of this made any sense. It was also very depressing. Even worse, my local GP at that time did not want to know, and made it quite evident when he called, by giving me a lecture on time wasting! So I tried to carry on, hoping that my condition would eventually improve. It didn't. Gradually, my arms and neck became immobile, and I was in such agony that I was beginning to look like a walking corpse. Michael Bentine visited me at that time, and did not think I would survive. Neither did I!

In the midst of all this I had to leave my home and find somewhere where I could take all the animals. Moving home at the best of times is dreadful, so you can imagine the trauma, especially as I could do nothing to help myself. I was also extremely miserable, as it was the first time in my life that I had rented someone else's home. It just did not feel right. I began to wonder what I had done to deserve this. And another thing. Where the hell was God!

I had spent the last two years making my healing room into a very lovely blue haven for all of my patients, and when I turned my back on it for the last time it felt just like leaving my home in Sutton all over again. I felt, yet again, that I had left a part of me behind.

Although my new home was set in lovely surroundings, the house itself was cold and uninviting. It was a typical rented house, and had not been used as a real home for years. I suppose I could have overcome this but I was racked with pain, and felt as though I had boiling oil in my chest and back. Lying in bed was a nightmare, as I could not shift from one position to another without further agony.

After five months, it became obvious to everyone concerned that something was terribly wrong. Apart from the pain, the black shadows that passed over my eyes were becoming more frequent, and lasting longer.

I visited my heart surgeon. He took one look at me and told me to book into the hospital the next day. I was so relieved.

When my second operation was over, my surgeon visited me and told me that he had had to remove every piece of the wire that had been used to join the sternum, as it had all corroded. I was told that it was very unusual for this to happen, as titanium, which is practically corrosive resistant, is used frequently in surgery for this reason. I later spoke to one or two scientist friends, who told me that the only thing that could do this to titanium was electricity, and that my healing power had obviously caused the damage. This all made sense to me. The electricity had caused a circuit, creating heat, which had eventually corroded the titanium and that was why it felt like boiling oil. I'm sure that I'm not the only person this has happened to, but it is certainly very rare. The transformation was immediate, and for the first time in five months my body was free of pain and I felt that I had a future.

Six weeks later I was on television promoting my book, and continued with the publicity tour. *Mind Waves* was a bestseller. All three books were bestsellers, in both hardback and paperback, and I know that I could never have achieved this without spiritual help and guidance.

There are many reasons why I have told you this part of my very private experience. One is that my readers all over the world have become part of my family, and love to hear the latest news. Also, at a time when they wanted to see more of me, they were seeing less; although I very rarely cancelled appointments, I had cut them down. I did not want to go public with my story at the time, as it would have taken away the peace and quiet that my family and I so desperately needed. As a result explanations were perhaps unsatisfactory, and left some people feeling they had been let down. Nothing could have been further from the truth. Janet and I worked all through that very difficult time, and the end results proved that we were on the right lines.

The second reason is far more important. I have received so many letters from people telling me that either they, or a member of their family, had decided against open heart surgery because they were too scared to face the operation. Even though I urged them to go through with it, there were some I could not reach, and they died. To this day, I cannot help thinking of the terrible waste of life. My own story was so unusual that it can be dismissed. The fact is that in two days you are up and about, and looking forward to a healthy future. The pain factor gradually decreases, and in three months you will know that it had all been worth it. There is also a great bonus. You come face to face with yourself, and realize that never again will you ever take your life for granted. Neither will you allow anyone to take you for granted.

If you have been told that you have to have heart surgery to save your life, take the gift with both hands, and thank God that it is available.

❦

CHAPTER TWENTY-TWO

I N A TELEPHONE CONVERSATION WITH A FRIEND, I spoke about the incredible help that I had received by using the exercises that were printed in my books. She told me that they had also helped her, but that it was time wasting having to looking through all three books to find a specific exercise. When she suggested that I put all the exercises into one book, *Betty Shine's Mind Workbook* was born. This was a brilliant idea, and I wondered why I hadn't thought of it myself. But I had been otherwise engaged!

I had by now received thousands of letters from around the world, with descriptions of the wonderful things that had happened to individuals and circles when they used these exercises. The most popular was the *Mind Medicine Room*. The successful 'mind' treatment that people were giving themselves in this room was fantastic, proving once again that we can either kill or cure ourselves with the power of our minds. By applying mind power to their specific ailments, diabetics – with the permission of their doctors – had been able to cut down their insulin. Those suffering with chronic arthritis had gradually cut their intake of painkillers, and had learnt to bypass the pain through meditation. Minor ailments by the score had responded to the 'mind' treatment, and hundreds suffering major problems had been able to back up their medical treatment by visiting their *Mind Medicine Room*. They told me that it gave them back their independence, and meant that they could once again control their own lives.

The healing circles that had been started with these exercises were extremely successful, and many people who had been unable to help themselves had found health, happiness and new friends.

I was regaled with stories of spirit sightings. This did not surprise me at all, for with the practice of mind expansion it becomes inevitable. What did surprise me, however, was the detailed description of 'dead' relatives, friends and pets, and the survival messages and clairvoyance that were given, which added to my conviction that with the right kind of application our minds can become a part of other dimensions. It is simply a question of 'knowing' that you can do it. But if there are any doubts at all, it simply will not happen. It is rather like riding a bicycle or swimming; once you have done it, you 'know' that you will always be able to do it.

I would like everyone to have this experience, but I know that we are living in a world where cynicism prevails, so I am realistic. But there is a psychic revolution taking place, and those who have had psychic experiences are finding the courage to speak out, no longer cowed by their antagonists. Some say that more children are being born psychic. I do not believe this. Children have always come into this world with psychic abilities – it is a vital part of our make-up – but in the past this was not understood and so the gift was quickly eliminated by parents, teachers and the church. To allow our psyche to work for us should be completely natural, as should the knowledge that we have spiritual companions who open us up to our natural talents and guide us through the maze of our lives from birth to death, and welcome us when we are reborn. It should be as natural as breathing, but it isn't, because we have been ruled by the ignorance of others. But times are changing and the children of today do not accept so readily the condemnations of their elders. They want to find out for themselves. They are interested in unusual experiences and, above all, they are more courageous in their attitude to life and death. The young ones are more compassionate because they can see for themselves, on television, the terrible acts of inhumanity that are acted out around the world. They will be our healers of the future.

CHAPTER TWENTY-THREE

WHEN I LOST MY HOME, I never gave up the hope that one day I would find somewhere that would give me the peace and contentment I needed. I knew I would have difficulties, because I would have to live in rented accommodation, but hope is eternal. Without it we are lost. I contacted someone who I thought might be able to help me, and was told that there was a farmhouse that had just been vacated. I asked Janet to accompany me, so that we could both tune into the vibrations of the place. Travelling along a narrow track, we passed a white house. Janet immediately grabbed my arm and pointed to the house, saying, 'That's your house, that is where you're going to live.' I laughed, and thought she was being fanciful, as it was obvious that the house was occupied. We carried on to the farm. I loved it, and spent some time wandering around the huge beamed rooms with their splendid polished wood floors. But this was not dream-time, and I just could not afford it. Janet was totally disinterested in the place and was wandering around outside muttering that it was not my house. When I explained my financial predicament to our guide, he told me there was a house on another part of this very beautiful country estate, that was about to be vacated, and that he would point it out on the way back. We followed behind as he drove back up the lane, and when he reached the white house he put his arm out of the car window and pointed to it. Janet was ecstatic, and hugged me. 'I told you so,' she said. 'I knew that was your house. It's almost identical to your home in Sutton.' Looking at the huge windows I could certainly see the similarities.

It was two months before we could actually look around the house, but it felt like a lifetime. The place was upside down, the large wood-panelled lounge being upstairs so that the view across the valley to the nearest village could be appreciated. It had everything I needed.

Over the next two years, this house and the surrounding hills, valleys and woods, gave me back my health and the knowledge that God had not deserted me. This was His gift, and a day never passes without my thanking Him.

So many times in our lives we believe that we have been cast aside, only to find that it was merely a way of getting rid of the dead wood so that the new can survive. It is a painful process, but it has to be done if we are to progress, and our spiritual guides are way ahead of us in deciding when this surgery is to be carried out.

I used to smile in the early days of my mediumship when I heard spiritualists say, 'If you work for spirits, they will work for you.' In my ignorance, this had seemed too pat, but, after twenty-two years as a medium, I have been very grateful to have been on the receiving end of that help. However, I should like to add a word of warning; if you live in expectations of rewards for the help you give, you might be disappointed. Every action and thought is evaluated, and there is no way one can con the system. If you are working for your own glorification then your talents will always remain mediocre. Self has to come last when you are working with those in other dimensions, because Universal Law dictates that only selfless actions will be recognized and rewarded, and that whatever we give out will return. That does not mean to say that we all have to live the lives of saints, because life is for living, but it does mean that when something unpleasant happens to us we have to be strong enough to take it on the chin. And that is not as easy as it sounds, for it usually happens when we are at our lowest ebb, so that it produces the utmost impact.

I always remember the words of my spiritual teacher, who said, 'The outcome of so much greed, cruelty and lack of spirituality will bring about the downfall of nations, but the sight of the innocents that are tossed by the wayside will bring about a spiritual revival that will change the face of the earth, and the spirits of those innocents will be the driving force behind the change.'

This message was given to me in 1981. Since then, I think you will agree, the reliability of this prophecy has been proven. There *is* a spiritual revival, and it has very little to do with religion, for it is our minds that are the essence behind this change. Ordinary people all over the world have suffered for too long for the sins of others, and now these ordinary people, myself included, are sending out the power to put an end to the evil that exists. In the end good must prevail, for there is nothing more powerful than love. And that love must extend not only to humans but also to animals, for the abuse that is meted out to them is sinful and can no longer be tolerated. We all have to help, and that help can be given physically, financially or through a talent. Those that cannot help in any of these ways can send loving and powerful thoughts of healing which will, in turn, join other like thoughts and create waves which will give birth to a new ocean of energy. This energy will play an important role in the survival of this planet. There is much to do and so very little time, if we are not to succumb to the after effects of the terrible evils that are committed every day in some part of the world. This is not a life, it is an existence that should not be tolerated, and we must play our part now, or for ever be forced to hide our faces with shame when we are confronted by future generations. They are our children, and we must fight so that they can live in a more spiritual environment, where they will be able to see the love that surrounds every living thing on this planet.

I have had to make many changes in my life. In 1994, it became patently obvious to myself and my family that I could not continue with my practice, give absent healing and write books, the latter being a full time job of its own. The tremendous response I had received world-wide after the publication of the books made the decision I had to make a whole lot easier, and softened the blow when I ceased to practise on a regular basis. There were times, at first, when I felt guilty, but that is a natural process one goes through when changes are made, and the fact that I could spend more time giving absent healing made me feel much better. Now I could concentrate on my special interest, the power of thought. As it has turned out, I could not have made a better choice; the success of absent healing has surpassed my expectations, and the books have so far been translated into five languages, including Japanese. This has opened up more horizons, and the messages are being received loud and clear.

If I thought that I was going to get away from the mediumship and contact healing altogether, I was very much mistaken. Family and friends keep me busy, and whenever I am entertaining, survival evidence is never far away. There have been times when the session has gone on for hours, leaving everyone concerned in no doubt that there is a life after death, and that they were very privileged to have experienced this for themselves. Even after all these years, I am amazed at the timing and accuracy of the communicators, who have obviously given the matter much thought before they contact me.

During the writing of this book I have been inspired by my spirit teachers. The usual phenomena that has become part and parcel of my writing has appeared, and I am now receiving messages. Although they do not make sense at the moment, I am sure they will in the future. And it would not surprise me, one day, to see the faces of my spirit friends appear on the screen of my word processor.

I have decided to link up with technicians and scientists to see if we can push back the barriers. Maybe nothing will happen, but if it does then you can be sure that I will write about it.

One of the strange things that happened with this book was when I was writing about my spiritual teacher, who I call the guru, because I do not know his identity. I had been working for about three hours, and decided to finish for the day. I pressed the 'save' key but instead of it reading Chpt2 at the bottom of the screen it had changed into OM. If you understand the workings of computers you will know that you have to make a file, it cannot suddenly appear. I went back to my word processor filing cabinet, and found that I not only had Chp2 with Backup but I also had OM with Backup. I know that OM is a very well known mantra used by Buddhists, but I wanted to know more so looked it up in the dictionary, this is what it said.

Hinduism – a sacred symbol typifying the three gods Brahma, Vishnu and Siva, who are concerned in the threefold operation of integration, maintenance, and disintegration.

The intrigue continues, and keeps me on my toes. Another strange happening occurred whenever I mentioned other spiritual teachers who had communicated with me. A box appeared on the screen, with the word *sages* in bold print. This is an extremely old fashioned word for a spiritual teacher, but the message was all the more powerful because of that, as it was one that I never thought about or used.

For the future, I am dedicated to writing books that will help humanity.

On a final note, I thought you might like to know that Sally the cat is now thirteen years old, and we are still together. Sometimes, when she is on my lap, she will sit bolt upright and look at something behind my chair. Her body completely rigid, she will stay that way until 'it' disappears.

Living on a country estate, has given her the feeling for the great outdoors, and she spends most of her time stalking pheasant and partridge. However, as they are much too big for her to tackle, she contents herself by catching smaller prey, mostly mice. Perhaps she is joined by her spirit friends. I hope so.

Tessa and Flossie are now twelve and eleven respectively, and also enjoying life.

In the company of the animals and my spirits, I am always busy, and grateful for the gifts that have been bestowed upon me. I am forever hopeful that I will live up to the expectations of my spirit mentors!

If you wish to receive absent healing or book and tape brochure, please write to the address below:

P.O. Box 1009
Hassocks
West Sussex
BN6 8XS

Please enclose a stamped, addressed envelope for a reply. Thank you.